BAIL AND PREVENTIVE DETENTION IN NEW YORK

Edward J. Shaughnessy

UNIVERSITY
PRESS OF
AMERICA

Copyright © 1982 by

University Press of America, Inc.

P.O. Box 19101, Washington, D.C. 20036

Library of Congress Cataloging in Publication Data

Shaughnessy, Edward J.
  Bail and preventive detention in New York.

  Bibliography: p.
  Includes index.
  1. Bail—New York (State)   2. Preventive detention—
New York (State)   I. Title.
KFN6157.5.S48   1982   345.747'072   81-40904
ISBN 0-8191-2574-1   347.470572
ISBN 0-8191-2575-X (pbk.)

Table of Contents

Chapter IX

List of Tables

Chapter IV (cont'd)

Forward

The writing and organization of this book are mine. I bear the burdens of proof and fault. There were many who generously contributed to whatever success this effort may have. Lawyers, judges, academicians, court personnel, police, Bondsmen and street people.

I am also particularly grateful to the following members of the judicial and legal profession: The Honorable David Ross, former Administrative Judge of the Criminal Court, City of New York; Justice Peter McQuillan, the Supreme Court; Mr. Charles O'Meara, Deputy Chief Administrator of the Criminal Court; Mr. James Ward, Chief Statistician of the Criminal Court; Mr. John Wallace, former Chief of the Office of Probation. I am particularly indebted to Mr. Louis B. Warren, secretary of the Homeland Foundation, Inc., and partner in the firm of Kelley, Drye, Warren, Clark, Carr and Ellis, whose encouragement and support both financially and individually, brought about the initial research. The following members of the legal profession have also rendered great assistance in the analysis of the legal aspects of this work: Mr. Patrick McGinley, Commissioner of Investigation, New York; William vanden Heuvel, former Chairman of the Board of Correction of the City of New York; Professor Harry Subin of the New York University Law School, Mr. Robert Kasanov, former Chief of the Criminal Division of the Legal Aid Society; Dr. Gerhardt O.W. Mueller chief of the Crime Prevention and Criminal Justice Section of the United Nations.

Donald H. Goff, Albert Hess, Eric Single, Anne Ranken and Frederic Suffet were invaluable for their criticism and support. Dr. Keith Hawkins, Wolfson College, Oxford and Dr. Keith Bottomley, University of Manchester, England shared with me their writings and reflections on bail as an Anglo-Saxon social and institutional process.

This book appeared first as a doctoral dissertation, <u>Bail: Examination of an Institutional Process in Criminal Court, New York County in 1973</u>. The study was directed by the late Professor Benjamin Nelson of the Department of Sociology, Graduate Faculty of the New School for Social Research. The text has been revised and updated. The librarians of New York University Library, Fordham University Law Library, the John Jay College of Criminal Justice Library, the New School for Social Research Library, and the Bienecke Library of the Yale University and the Millbrook Free Library extended themselves many times for me. Particular thanks are due to Mary A. Keelan, Director, Media and Scholars Associates, for analysis and critique of the contents of this book, for offering resources and the material on the Middle Ages and for all of the patience and endurance which accompany her role in life. I am lastly and deeply indebted to Doris DeVito who produced faithfully and diligently the entire manuscript. The index was prepared by Dolores Grande.

Introduction

The last twenty years have seen an attack upon the administration of criminal justice in the United States of America unparalleled in its history. The legal shortcomings, the social faults, the corruptions, the irregularities and the miscarriages have become the stuff of social scientists and soap operas. There is and can be no question that the discoveries of defect were long overdue. The administration of criminal justice has problems enumerated and exorcised elsewhere. This book takes a look at one of the "whipping boys" of the criminal justice system, bail. Bail: the pledge of assets - cash or kind - to the court to guarantee the appearance of a defendant in a criminal action when required by the court. Bail was seen as symptomatic of the ills of the system of criminal justice. If you had wealth you could "buy" your pretrial freedom. If you were poor you languished in detention while awaiting trial. As our criminal courts arraigned more offenders it became clearer and clearer that the majority, more than 80% today, are poor, minorities lacking in the social resources; jobs, education and skills needed to "make a go of it" in the middle class world of America. Clearly there was and is a problem. Leftist thinkers, Marxist and Socialist, saw the classic exploitation of the sub-structure, the proletariat by the superstructure, the capitalist. Populists and libertarians articulated the contradiction between the democratic principles of equality articulated in our Declaration of Indedpendence and The Constitution reminding us that the theory was not showing up in practice. The Supreme Court in the decade of the 1950s was a hall-mark in constitutional consciousness raising. Even the conservatives, those who cherish the roots of our society and its institutions had to recognize that all was not well with the body of criminal law and procedure.

A concerted effort was launched against the court's administration of criminal law - right to counsel, right to silence, right to transcripts, right to protection against unlawful search, right to a speedy trial, right to correction, treatment or rehabilitation and a right to bail. Because bail came so early in the pre-trial and arraignment process it became a critical focus, for as a bail decision went, so went the case, to sum up Patricia Wald's view of it in 1963. Hence a defendant's chance to a fair adjudication was contingent on what happened to him at bail.

The problem, of course, was and still is, what is bail supposed to be? Is it an absolute constitutional right or not? What is bail supposed to do? Does it secure a defendant and prevent his flight from the court's jurisdiction or does it punish him before he has been convicted of a crime? What are the grounds for bail? Should some persons be detained regardless of this right to bail?

There is no constitutional right to bail. The United States and New York State Constitutions provide only that bail, if granted, shall not be "excessive." Nevertheless, even a minimal bail may often prove excessive for many indigent and presumably innocent defendants. Recognizing this, most legal commentators have concluded that the money bail system, as utilized in New York, is discriminatory, inequitable and unconstitutional. It is undeniably not in conformity with modern concepts of criminal and social justice.

Could bail be other than monetary and if so, what? Finally, how can we be sure that a defendant who falls prey to the wiles of a bail bondsman, "the bete noire" of criminal court, will not be just another victim of injustice. These are the questions which were hurled at bail conferences in those twenty years from 1960 to 1980 - few of those questions have been answered with any finality. The result of the questioning has made bail the locus of the onslaught of reform - a symbol of abuse, a practice nefarious and suspect which should be approached with caution.

The effect of this onslaught has been to take a useful tool in the criminal justice system, a practice enduring over a thousand years, and make it both disreputable and dysfunctional. This book will look at how this state of affairs came to be.

The conclusions, are based upon a study of selected defendants in New York City Criminal Court. Recommendations include the establishment of a separate bail part in the criminal court at which a point system developed from weighted criteria would be applied to the issue of the defendant's release. The point score

would not bind the judge to release or detain; however,
it would enable him to exercise a proper and informed
judicial discretion.

CHAPTER I

THE EVOLUTION OF BAIL FROM
MEDIEVAL TO MODERN PRACTICE

Historical Foundations

The awareness of justice as the outcome of an adversarial procedure is as old as man. An entire work should be given to the rationalization of the adversarial contest in the framework of the law, but for our purposes the concern is with the decision to grant bail as an aspect of rational adversarial procedure.

An analysis of the Anglo-Saxon or 10th century bail practices will give the reader a sense of the customary "binding over to keep the peace" in this period. It was on such usage that later Anglo-Norman bail practice was built.[1]

In England there was little need for bail as long as justice was swift, but once the system of government became centralized and trial courts replaced trial by ordeal, the need for bail arose. Bail was part of the adversarial procedure in that a person had to "argue" a case for release and, when released on bail, had to conform to certain rules of conduct, or perform certain deeds until the appointed day of judgment.

The year 1100 was a benchmark in the evolution of bail practice. Prior to this time, before the establishment of Norman rule the customs were quite different.

The Surety in Anglo-Saxon Customary Law

In the Anglo-Saxon period a "wergeld" payment, a type of victim compensation, was to be paid by the kin of the defendant/debtor. This practice of "Wer" payment replaced seizure and the feud as a form of victim compensation. The interim period between the incident and its resolution by wergeld payment appears to have been lengthy. Thus it became necessary to arrange for a kind of three-fold surety: for the defendant, for the complainant, for payment. This tended to avoid frivolous charges and to assure that parties would abide by any agreement reached.

The Anglo-Saxon suretyship system involved: first, payment of the wergeld to the sib or kin group; second, the payment of the "wite" which was in payment to authority for bloodshed; third, because most men were bound to a lord, the payment of the "manbot" to the lord, for the disturbance of the peace of the land. In essence all of these were done in one contract,

according to rules of procedure which evolved into a
determinate social structure. Given the presence of a
victim and a defendant in a tightly knit social structure of a tribe or clan, the role of intermediaries
became clear. The intermediary for the defendant, a
kinsman or other, offered sureties for the payment of
the wergeld, which were called the "werborh." In
return the intermediary for the victim offered surety
of safety that the victim's kin would not assault the
defendant and would permit him to go about in peace.
Once this contract was made, a direct meeting, if
possible, was arranged between the defendant and the
victim or his kin, at which time a symbolic pledge of
responsibility, an acknowledgment of guilt called the
"wed" was made. This symbol was then given to the
principal surety, usually that of the defendant, who
was called the "borh."

Actions committed against members of the community
or tribe were not crimes, as we know them, implying a
responsibility to the state, but crimes in the sense
defined by Emile Durkheim,[2] i.e. those acts abhorred by
all members of a society. The offenses considered here
took place on a private level, principally as pleas
between families, but there was a recognition of a
wider disruption of the peace symbolized by payment of
the "manbot." It is with the start of centralization
of authority around 1100 that the beginning of wider
responsibility is assigned to the state and the
institution of crown pleas commences to evolve.

The Rationalization of Bail Procedure

The 12th and 13th centuries were the seedbed of
modern European society. Authorities such as Benjamin
Nelson[3] have drawn our attention to this "mini-
renaissance." "It was," according to Nelson, "exactly
the differentiation into kingdoms, principalities,
cities, estates (stande), professions, universities and
so on which help us understand the extraordinary pulse-
beat of the developments of the 12th and 13th
centuries." This was the time for sifting and collating
critical traditions in law and science and philosophy.
England may have been somewhat slower than the continent
in jurisprudence, but with Bracton[4] and Edward I, the
codifier, we find two systematic synthesizers. The
movement toward rationalization was under way at Oxford
with Robert Grosseteste, William of Heytesbury, and
Thomas of Bradwardine. The hallmark of the 12th and
13th centuries in Anglo-Norman law is the focus on

orientations and institutions, according to Nelson, which simultaneously rests upon two-fold commitment to the individual and the objective universal. The main premise on which institutions are raised is that individuated persons are the bearers of rights and rationalized universals become the focal points of governing norms.

Henry Sumner Maine in his <u>Ancient Law</u>[5] shows the surge in the 13th and 14th centuries toward the expansion of those qualified to be (often status?) persons in their own right, i.e. passage from status, to contract, to individual rights. As will be shown, the laws governing sureties and pretrial release are indicative of this passage.

Surety in early Anglo-Saxon procedure was related to a particular offense, and, as Vinogradoff states,[6] the Wergeld was not designed to be paid by an individual. Therefore when, after the Norman Conquest in 1066,[7] the "maegath" or kinship bond had loosened, "bail" surety consisted of someone not a member of the family, but rather a friend or individual not chosen in advance. In this weakened kinship structure, the family or "maegas" was less likely to make the wergeld payment.

Gierke found the origin of bail in hostageship. "Suretyship is incorporeal hostageship, <u>ideele vergeiselung</u>, which is an obvious result of an evolutionary process from hostageship itself. . . ."[8] Initially the surety assumed the liability as a kind of trustee. Later, under the Normans, the surety became, a guarantor of a different kind, one who was prepared to redeem the pledge.

The Norman Influence

Under the laws of Henry I, "wer," "manbot," and "wite" payments gradually disappeared. Afflictive punishment and the ordeal were substituted until outlawed by the Lateran Council in 1215, whose decision took nearly a century to implement.

Monetary consequences developed upon a surety in both Anglo-Saxon and Norman periods where default occurred. The establishment of a frankpledge system was a final step in evolutionary suretyship. Based upon Anglo-Saxon institutions, it was an adaptation, made compulsory, mutual and collective, of the association of ten. Frankpledge did not assure presence in court. Rather, it was an all inclusive arrangement whereby a group, engaged in the mutual supervision of the members of the association, made arrests of members who infringed the law before action could be taken by the authorities. According to Morris, it was a kind of collective responsibility in anticipation of the commission of a crime. However, an individual or selected individuals functioned as sureties for appearance at trial when an offense did occur. It was the function as "borh ' which developed into the individual "plegium" and appeared as the writ de homine replegiando.[9]

There is a clear relationship between the social structures of the wergeld payment as described earlier and the type of pledging found in Piperolls,[10] where pledges had to be presented on behalf of the accuser and the accused as well as witnesses if any.

Prior to 1166, there were two categories of offenses, i.e. those replevisable under common law and those irreplevisable. After the Assize of Clarendon in 1166, the transition was from individuals taking private action to crown pleas or rules established by the state. The writ de homine replegiando probably existed as early as 1170 but writs 'de odio et atia and de ponendo did not exist prior to 1227. Three noteworthy occasions were: first, the establishment of a definite class of felons of royal concern i.e. "robbers, murderers or thieves or receivers of them" (1166); second, the Assize of Northampton (1176) which added arson and forgery, and established the presentment jury which initiated prosecution, thereby increasing frequency of bail cases; and third, introduction of justices in eyre, i.e. local magistrates who admitted to bail.

The Normans brought trial by combat which is a variety of the general legal proceeding of ordeal which seems to have been confined to the Germanic peoples. Ordeal is a formal test or test employed under some fixed conditions to determine the will of God, the gods, the death or fate in a matter of some importance, often involving innocence or guilt, for human beings. It is most usually associated with determining the guilt of a person or truth of a claim in order that justice be done, but not always or necessarily. The guilt ordeals are the most dramatic but not the only ones. There are three types of ordeal according to their aims: first, the neutral, as when arrows are shot to determine which road to take (Ezekiel xxi, 21), or when lots are cast for the selection of an official or in the choice of a sacrificial animal; second, the truth of the property or ownership of a claim is a type of ordeal; and third, guilt or innocence when a charge is preferred against someone. This last may be subdivided into unilateral ordeals when fire, water swallowing, lots are used on a suspected violator, and multilateral when battle decides the issue. It appears that the Normans brought trial by combat to England, around 1066.

Trial by ordeal in combat was a method used to get at the truth when oaths would not elicit the answer. Accusations could not simply be dismissed, an answer had to be given. Ordeals were salutary in that they were decisive.[11] Trial by combat was undoubtedly a forward step in the development of trial procedures as it put under some kind of order and ritual a method which was no doubt used at random - the use of force to settle disputes. Ordeal by combat survived a long time. It favored the strong and could claim divine sanction.

As the government of England became more central-ized and laws regulated and controlled the conduct of men, the use of trial by combat found a more congenial place in the courtly tradition of knighthood where the test of strength was a test of virtue, and the trial by ordeal became a time-consuming challenge which required the liberty of the challenger and the chal-lenged to complete the ordeal.[12] It is difficult, though not impossible, to reconstruct the data for actual pretrial practices in the medieval period of history. What we can find are hints from documents which suggest what risks the society was prepared to take and how the costs of pretrial administration were allocated at any given time.

The Statute of Westminster the First, 1275, which provided a substantial list of offenses which were bailable even though together with a longer enumeration of non-bailable crimes, also suggests at least a certain liberality. Indeed, indications are in 13th and 14th century England that pretrial detention was actually rarely used. Pollack and Maitland in their History of English Law note

> It was not common to keep men in prison.
> This apparent leniency of our law was not
> due to any love of the abstract liberty.
> Imprisonment was costly and troublesome. . . .
> and there were many ways out of it. . . .[13]

The usual way of handling those accused felons was to turn over responsibility for their handling to their friends. It is difficult to draw firm conclusions from this evidence about how English bail policy worked at this period. Not only were the most seriously accused excluded because of the proliferation of capital crimes, but primitive procedures for dealing with persons accused removed many more from the pretrial population. In 1275 both outlawry and the hue and cry were still extant; in the 13th century this hue and cry form of justice rid England of more malefactors than the courts could hang according to Pollock and Maitland. Under these conditions the question of what to do with a man between arrest and trial was moot because there was no pretrial period to speak of, and virtually no trial, the culprit being dispatched promptly. A society can engage in the luxury of a bail procedure if it is certain that all the really dangerous and obviously guilty defendants have been dispatched previously. In any event, the bail legislation in the statute books probably bore little relation to the actualities of bail practice. Perhaps the most interesting insights into how the law was circumvented is found in an article by Thomas A. Green entitled "Societal Concepts of Criminal Liability for Homicide in Medieval England." In Green's analysis of homicide cases he says

> The new 12th century practice subjected to the death penalty not only 'murderers' but the large class of open slayers formerly allowed to compensate for their act by the payment of the wergeld. The community resisted this harsh extension of capital punishment and subsequently found means - acquittals and verdicts of self-defense - to impose upon the courts their long-held notions of justice, a process which becomes visible to us only as of the 14th century . . . .Nor did the imposition of the new scheme of criminal administration prevent society from acting, within the context of that scheme, in accordance with its traditional attitudes.[14]

Later we shall see that by the time of the American Revolution, English bail law was a tangled mess. The basic Statute of Westminster the First of 1275 provided the detailed enumeration of what offenses sheriffs must bail or could not bail, and remained the basic guideline for five and a half centuries. It represented a

reaction against abuses which had developed under
earlier law which gave sheriffs discretion whether or
not to admit to bail. In the succeeding centuries many
statutes were added and bail was transferred from the
sheriff to the justice of the peace, as Parliament
sought to check illegal bailing of non-bailable offenders. This particular aspect of regulation is brought
out in Sir Edward Coke's treatise entitled A Little
Treatise of Baile and Maineprize, published in 1637.[15]
Such English bail statutes were important models in the
struggle which shaped our criminal procedure. As will
be seen, the statutory pattern of English law was
reinforced in the Petition of Right, the Habeas Corpus
Act and the Excessive Bail Clause of the Bill of Rights
of 1689. In the medieval period justice administered
in the eyre and the hundred[16] remained swift and suspects were, as noted, rarely detained.[17] Detention
became a problem when certain crimes were reserved to
the Crown for resolution in the king's court. This
required the presence of the king's justice in the
region, and the suspects were held for such sessions
or released on the pledge of surety. The Anglo-
American bail system is rooted in this legal practice
of controlling the accused in his region pending
trial.[18] It was rarely in its inception an instrument
for detention, since flight was highly unlikely due to
the close-knit nature of the communities and the
penalties for flight.[19]

The Centralization of Medieval Justice

Bail has origins in the medieval practice of
wergeld, a tax or fine paid to obtain release when one
has been charged with a crime and convicted.[20] The
institutionalization of such a practice appears with
the Assize of Clarendon in 1166. The institution of
the pleas of the Crown, the presentment jury, itinerant
justices and the creation of the court, the Sheriff's
Tourne at which the sheriff was authorized to release
or hold the accused, were all offspring of Clarendon.
"Originally the functions of bail appear to have been
to lighten the custodial duties of the sheriff and to
avoid having prisoners starve to death before their
case could be heard."[21] In the early years of Norman
order, which suffered from deplorable jails, itinerant
justices and infrequent trials, the sheriff generally
exercised discretion in determining the release of a
prisoner on his honor or to the custody of a third
party who would assure the accused's appearance for
trial. If the potential defendant escaped, the third
party had to surrender himself.

> Thou shalt besiek hem alle
>   To bring theee out of bondes;
> And if they will borwe three,
>   That were good game;
> Then were thou out of prisoun
>   And I out of blame.[22]

The ever-increasing corruption of the sheriffs as they exercised their discretion in bailing those accused led to the Statute of Westminster the First which standardized the practices of bail by enumerating the non-bailable offenses and authorizing justices rather than sheriffs to make the bail determination. Passed in 1275, the Statute of Westminster was the basis of the British bail system for 550 years. This Statute grouped detainees into two categories.

> Every wrong or trespass against the peace of the King although the offense reached a felony, everyone that is appealed or indicted is wanted to be Bailed - except only in the case of the death of a man. . . .[23]

In one category bail was a matter of right and in the other bail was not allowed.

The personal exposure of the surety was usually deemed a better guarantee of the continued presence of the accused in the jurisdiction than the loosely guarded prisons of that time.[24] Bracton, in The Laws and Customs of England,[25] emphasizes the importance of pledges as the instrumentality for securing release on bail. Throughout the entire second volume of Thorne's translation of Bracton are interlaced references to the bailability of defendants as early as 1175, when Bracton first published his commentary.

In 1628, the Petition of Right afforded to pre-trial detention the guarantees of the 39th Chapter of the Magna Carta. The Great Charter provided that "no free man shall be arrested, or detained in prison. . . unless. . .by the law of the land."[26] The Habeas Corpus Act of 1679 provided for release of those who were unjustly detained before trial since "many of the king's subjects have been and hereafter may be long detained in prison, in such cases where by law they are bailable. . . ."[27] However, judges continued to set impossibly high bail in many cases, with the result that the Preamble to the Bill of Rights of 1689 stated: "Excessive bail hath been required of persons committed

9

in criminal cases, to elude the benefit of the laws made
for the liberty of the subjects."[28]   Accordingly, the
English Bill of Rights provided "that excessive bail
ought not to be required. . . ."[29]

The first explication of the history and usage of
bail since the Middle Ages was Sir Edward Coke's A
Little Treatise of Baile and Maineprize, published in
1637.[30] Coke's opening sentence in Chapter 1 is a
definition of bail, as from the French bailer, to de-
liver. This definition has been taken by Goldfarb[31]
and Botein[32] as the origin of the word, which has its
roots in an old English word. The word bail comes from
the word borg[33] and the Middle English boirwe,[34] a noun
meaning pledge or bail. There is a body of literature
called "The Matter of England" which is a group of
Middle English romances expressive of themes of social
and historical value. In these romances the Middle
English word Boirwe is used. In the Gamelyn Romance[35]
the expression, "they will borwe thee. . . ." is translated "they will go bail for you. . . ."[36] As the
Gamelyn poet put it in lines 735 through 752:

        'Sire,'saide Sire Ote   to the sherreve tho,
        'We been but three bretheren- shull we never be mo-
        And thou hast y-prisoned the best of us alle;
         Swiche another brother ivel mot him bifalle.!'
        'Sir Ote,'saide the fals knight, 'lat be thy curs;
         By God, for thy wordes, he shall fare the wurs!
         To the kinges of prisoun anon he is y-nome
         And ther he shall abide   til the justice come.'
        'Par de!'said Sir Ote,   'better it shall be;
        *I bidde him to mainpris   that thou graunt him me
         Till the next sitting of deliverance
         And thanne lat Gamelyn   stande to his chaunce.'
        'Brother, in swich a forthward, I take him to thee;

         And by thy fader soule   that thee bigat and me,
         But-if he be redy   when the justice sitte,
         Thou shalt bere the judgement for all they grete
                                                    witte.'
        'I graunte well,'said Sir Ote,   that it so be.
         Let deliver him anon   and take him to me.'

    *(744 I demand (or ask) bail for him.[37]

        For I am under borwe,
            Til that I come
        And my brother for me
            To prisoun shall be nomed.[38]

                        10

Three centuries elapsed between the Gamelyn poet and the time Sir Edward Coke wrote his treatise, and it was another three centuries before Arthur L. Beeley wrote, in 1927 <u>The Bail System in Chicago</u>,[39] which was the first attempt to explore the alternatives to jail detention available to defendants. Those three centuries between Coke and Beeley have brought innumerable modifications to the operation of the bail system.

The Legal Foundations of Bail in America

The American constitutional question concerns itself with first, the nature and meaning of the right to bail; second, what is excessive; and third, the social implications of bail.

The studies which have been made in the last twenty years have established three things which, when they finally find their way into litigation, will pose major constitutional questions. First, it has been demonstrated the pretrial imprisonment of the poor as a result of their poverty under harsher conditions than those applied to convicted prisoners, so pervades our system that for a majority of defendants accused of anything more serious than petty crimes the bail system operates effectively to deny rather than facilitate liberty pending trial.[40] Second, it also is apparent that were it not for their poverty, a significant number of these jailed defendants would never be imprisoned because they are either not convicted or the disposition of their cases does not include imprisonment.[41] Third, there is an extraordinary correlation between pretrial status and the severity of the sentence after conviction, the jailed defendant being two or three times more likely to receive a prison sentence. The last finding raises difficult problems in evaluation because it is possible that there may be some other variable causing both pretrial jail status and severe sentence, although this book and the study of the Legal Aid Society indicate that the ratio holds constant even when obvious major variables are controlled.[42] While it would be preferable that the administration of criminal justice would accomplish a more equitable resolution of the pretrial disposition of the defendant without having a major court contest to accomplish this, there is no indication that this will be done without a Supreme Court decision.

It is important to keep in mind that if defendants are kept incarcerated, the cost is borne by those among them who are innocent or prejudiced by this detention.

If they are all released, society pays in those cases where the defendant flees or commits a new crime.[43] In theory, our system inclines to the second alternative. As Justice Jackson said in the decision St́ack vs. Boyle, "The spirit of the '/bail7 procedure is to enable. . . /defendants7 to stay out of jail until a trial has found them guilty."[44]This is the risk which the law takes as the price for our criminal justice system. American law actually puts most of the cost upon the shoulders of those who are detained and not upon society. The concept that the accused person should not be punished prior to a finding of guilty has deep roots in our culture with no fully comparable history in Europe.[45]

This policy problem is further complicated by the uncertain status of bail in the Federal Constitutional system. Standing alone, the excessive bail clause of the 8th Amendment poses puzzling questions of interpretation and historical analysis. As applied to indigents, any rights alleged under the 8th Amendment overlap broader due process and equal protection claims inherent in the financial discrimination and prejudice of the bail system. One indulges the assumption that current financial discrimination in bail cannot survive in the current renaissance of equal justice for the poor, that it makes a critical difference whether the court finds a resolution of the problem in interpretation which reads the 8th Amendment as including the right to pretrial release, or on the other hand, bypasses the 8th Amendment and fashions a less sweeping and more flexible due process and equal protection remedy. Thus, we must ask the question, does the 8th Amendment carry a right to bail? This book suggests that constitutionally the particular form in which the bail question appears is the result of historical evolution and accretion rooted in the Middle Ages, which we have discussed before. It is plausible to resolve this problem to find an intention to grant a right to bail. Also, assuming a right to bail, what meaning is to be attached constitutionally in the case of indigents to the requirement that bail shall not be excessive?

The Right to Bail

The importance of bail in order to avoid pretrial imprisonment was a central theme in the promise made in Chapter 39 of the Magna Carta: "No free man shall be arrested, or detained in prison. . .unless. . .by the

law of the land."[46]   It is important to keep in mind
that the three most critical steps in the formation of
this norm in modern practical application are the
Petition of Right of 1628, the Habeas Corpus Act of
1679, and the Bill of Rights of 1689.   These grew out
of cases which alleged denial of freedom pending trial.
The cases can be found in summation in the writings of
Professor Caleb Foote.[47]

It is important to note that English protection
against pretrial detention evolved to include three
separate and essential elements.   The first was the
determination of whether a given defendant had the
right to release on bail, answered by the Petition of
Right, by a long line of statutes which spelled out
which cases must and must not be bailed by justices of
the peace or the sheriffs according to Sir Edward Coke,
and the discretionary powers of the judges of King's
Bench to bail any case not bailable by lower judiciary.
Second was the simple effect of habeas corpus procedure
which developed to convert into reality rights derived
from legislation which could otherwise be thwarted.
Third was the protection against judicial abuse provided by the Excessive Bail Clause of the Bill of
Rights of 1689.   This protective structure, like
Montesquieu's system of balances in The Spirit of Laws,
formed the basis for the American bail system.[48]

The American transposition of this English system
of protection lacked a certain balance.   This is the
heart of the federal constitutional problem.   The
principle of habeas corpus found its way into Article I,
Section 9 of the Constitution, while the excessive bail
language of the 1689 Bill of Rights was included in the
8th Amendment.   But the underlying right to the remedy
of bail itself which these enactments supplemented and
guaranteed, was omitted.   Thus removed from its English
historical context and standing incomplete, the excessive bail clause of the 8th Amendment represents some
of the most ambiguous language in the Bill of Rights.
It is susceptible to three interpretations.   The first
interpretation is: bail cannot be demanded in an excessive sum in cases made bailable by other provisions
of law, but the clause itself imports no right to
bail.[49]   Such an interpretation, supposes that a
constitutional provision, being merely auxiliary to
some other law which in the federal system must be
statutory, requires one to believe that a basic human
right would be deliberately inserted in a constitution
in a form which permitted Congress to restrict it at

13

will, or even to render the 8th Amendment entirely moot
by enacting legislation denying the right to bail in all
cases. Such legislative power is consistent with the
English theory of civil liberties, in which Parliament
itself is the ultimate authority from which there is no
other protection. But it would be anomalous in the
American Bill of Rights whose central concern was
protection against abuse by Congress. The difficulty
is compounded when one recalls that the other clauses
in the 8th Amendment, no excessive fines and no cruel
and unusual punishment, traditionally have been interpreted to protect against abuse of legislative but not
of judicial discretion. The problem of such patently
incomplete constitutional protection on the subject of
bail led most states to supplement the excessive bail
clause by a clause granting right to bail in all non-
capital cases. The same anomaly would become acute in
the federal system if the 8th Amendment clause were
held applicable to the states through the 14th Amendment. Since the federal statutory right to bail could
not be incorporated for this purpose, the court would
have to adopt one of the following alternative interpretations. This requires us to look at a second
interpretation of the 8th Amendment.

Bail cannot be demanded in an excessive amount in
cases in which the court sets bail, but in the absence
of other statutory or constitutional restriction the
court retains discretion to deny bail altogether. This
interpretation fails to give effective protection even
against judicial action, let alone legislative abuse.
By making the clause say that the bail set in court may
not do indirectly what it is, however, permitted to do
directly - deny release - the clause is reduced to the
stature of little more than a pious platitude. If this
is what the clause means, any purported application
of it to the states would amount to a meaningless
formality. Another alternative interpretation is that
the excessive bail clause implies a constitutional
right to bail. This frequently-stated interpretation
has been reached as a necessary implication of the
difficulty of alternatives posed above. It may be the
interpretation most consistent with historical evolution of the 8th Amendment. One problem with the
approach is that the precise bounds of the "right" are
undefined; does it apply in capital cases, on appeal
to dangerous offenders, to what? More difficult is
the objection that if the founders of the Constitution
intended by the 8th Amendment to establish a right to
bail in all or most cases, why didn't they say so?

They had ample colonial precedents for a forthright
declaration in the Massachusetts Body of Liberties of
1641.[50] Indeed, only two years before the Bill of
Rights was debated in Congress, the Continental Congress
had inserted as one of the protections enacted as part
of the ordinance to govern the Northwest Territory a
bail guarantee, which omitting reference to excessive
bail, provided that all persons shall be bailable,
unless for capital offenses where the proof shall be
evident or the presumption great.[51] This language
found its way into the Judiciary Act[52] which was debated
in the First Congress concomitantly with the debate on
the Bill of Rights. While it is difficult to establish
direct evidence relevant to the circumstances and
philosophy governing the interpretation of bail in this
country at the time it was written into law, much can
be learned from the examination of the 8th Amendment
clause in legal interpretation. Contemporary American
and English bail law is also significant in ascertaining the probable intention behind the use of the clause,
and it is highly relevant to any attempt to accommodate
the language of the Amendment to the policy problems of
current criminal justice and its administration.[53]

   The classic 19th century bail case involved a
Mr. Lawrence arrested in 1835 after firing two pistols
at President Jackson in the Capitol Rotunda. Lawrence
was brought before Chief Judge Cranch, who "supposed
bail in $1,000 would be sufficient, as it was not a
penitentiary offense, there being no actual battery,
and as he did not appear to have any property." When
the district attorney objected that if the defendant
were released he might try again,

> The Chief Judge then said that there was
> no evidence before him to induce a sus-
> picion that any other person was concerned
> in the act; that the Constitution forbade
> him to require excessive bail; and that to
> require larger bail than the prisoner could
> give would be to require excessive bail and
> to deny bail in a case clearly bailable by
> law. . . .That the discretion of the Magistrate
> in a criminal case is to be guided by the
> compound consideration of the ability of
> the prisoner to give bail, and the atrocity
> of the offense. That as the prisoner had
> some reputable friends who might be disposed
> to bail him he would require bail in the sum
> of $1500. This sum, if the ability of the

> prisoner alone were considered, is, probably,
> too large; but if the atrocity of the offense
> alone were considered might seem to small.54

The opinion is ambiguous as to whether $1000 was design-
ed to make it possible or impossible for Lawrence's
friends to bail him; in either event, the bail issue
was moot when he was committed on ground of insanity.
But the court recognized the dilemma posed by the 8th
Amendment and its opinion might have launched further
analysis of the problem. However, very few cases in
the next 125 years addressed the issue of bail.55

Soon after the Cranch case, Alexis de Toqueville
discussing some of the anomalies he found in America,
wrote:

> No man can entirely shake off the influence
> of the past; and the settlers, intentionally
> or not, mingled habits and notions derived
> from their education and the traditions of
> their country with those habits and notions
> which were exclusively their own. . . .

> I shall quote a single example to illustrate
> my meaning. The civil and criminal procedure
> of the Americans has only two means of action,
> - committal or bail. The first act of the
> magistrate is to exact security from the
> defendant, or, in case of refusal, to in-
> carcerate him. . . .

> It is evident that such legislation is hostile
> to the poor and favorable only to the rich.
> The poor man has not always a security to
> produce even in a civil case and if he is
> obliged to wait for justice in prison, he is
> speedily reduced to distress. . . .56

There are only scattered references in 20th
century writings on bail, to the impact of the system
upon the poor. Even such a study as the Cleveland
Crime Survey of 1920-22 directed by Dean Pound and
Felix Frankfurter was inexplicably silent on the social
efficacy of the bail system as measured by the proportion of defendants who obtained pretrial freedom.57
One of the most disturbing manifestations of misdirec-
tion in the reformation of bail has been associated
with the preoccupation of reformers with bail
bondsmen.58

Under existing bail law the hypothetical defendant has very small chance of achieving immediate release
without financial secutiry. As will be seen, the
federal rule of Stack vs. Boyle is generally applied to
the states as well: bail in any amount usually fixed
for the crime charged is not deemed excessive. Individualized standards for bail setting, for example,
in the Federal Rules of Criminal Procedure, Rule #46,
apparently do not apply, and in practice are not
applied where bail is set in average amounts.[59]

The Stack vs. Boyle case, although not referring
to indigents, does show the implications of excessivity
in bail. The twelve Smith Act conspiracy defendants
did not allege in this particular case that they were
indigent; rather, each objected that bail had been set
in the uniform amount of $50,000 for the illegitimate
purpose of assuring that they would remain in jail.
Apparently envisaging an individualized procedure, the
court sent the cases back so that a hearing might be
held for reasonable bail for each defendant. The
Supreme Court opinion gave constitutional sanction
under the 8th Amendment to Rule 46 of Federal Procedure
that the amount is to be such as to insure the presence
of the defendant and that anything more presumably
exacted for any other purpose, is excessive. But
neither the Court's opinion nor that of Justice Jackson
was calculated to advance the position of those who
were indigent. The Court stated that the basic
standard to be applied is the amount usually fixed for
serious charges of crime. On the other hand, Justice
Jackson noted that if the unusually high bail were set
merely to keep the defendants in jail, it is contrary
to the whole philosophy of bail. He then added, "This
is not to say that every defendant is entitled to such
bail as he can provide, but he is entitled to an
opportunity to make it in a reasonable amount."[60]
There seems to be implied that bail set in the average
amount is reasonable and that individualization is required only for amounts greater than the average. This
also seems to be the most plausible explanation in
earlier cases. The effect of Stack vs. Boyle is to
leave the court free to establish minimum scales and
the evidence is overwhelming that this is in fact what
has been done. What this establishes clearly to
the detriment of the defendant is that the process
of averaging the bail amount prevents any violation of
the law because once the average amount of bail for a
particular crime has been established, then the

individual circumstances of the defendant are not required for consideration.

What we must see now is the necessity to move beyond the decision of Stack vs. Boyle to theories of due process which, although frequently applied in other areas of the law, have never been invoked in the field of bail, and an attempt to tie the 8th Amendment and equal protection theories which explicitly invite the courts to create new law, notwithstanding strong historical tradition otherwise. Thus it would be helpful to state specifically the aspects of a typical defendant's case. First, he is being denied the fundamental fairness guaranteed by due process of law because, although he alleges he is innocent, he is being punished by imprisonment before trial. Second, he is being denied procedural due process because detention adversely affects the disposition of his case. Third, he is denied equal protection of the law because on account of his financial circumstances he is denied pretrial liberty. Fourth, his right to bail under 8th and 14th Amendments is being violated because the proscription against "excessive bail" must be construed in such a way as not automatically to foreclose for indigents the fundamental right of freedom pending trial. There are two themes in all of these aspects of the defendant's position. First is the underlying value of a democratic administration of justice which is central to due process of law. Second is the dignity of man which is denigrated by procedures that fail to respect the intrinsic worth of the individual as a human person.

Justice Hugo Black in the Griffin vs. Illinois case[61] said, "There can be no equal justice when the kind of trial a man gets depends on the amount of money he has." But the power of the Griffin case resided in its ability to open areas of question which had not been explored before. In 1956 the Supreme Court decided in Griffin vs. Illinois that indigents could not be deprived of the benefits of a state system of appellate review by a requirement that appellants purchase and submit a transcript of the trial. This case arose because Griffin claimed that as a poor person he had no funds to purchase such a transcript and therefore was denied due process and equal protection of the law. The courts found in his favor and transcripts had to be provided. But one of the interesting aspects in the whole development of civil liberties in America has been the compartmentalization

18

which is found in a case like <u>Griffin</u> vs. <u>Illinois</u>. In this case we note that an indigent could not be refused what was necessary for the successful prosecution of his case, whereas we find there is no translation of this premise into the category of pretrial release. Similar analogies might be offered in the new confession standards also.[62]

While it is important that we bear in mind that no constitutional question is exclusively pertinent to the poor, the issues go beyond matters of wealth and poverty. What is significant in both Griffin and in <u>Stack</u> vs. <u>Boyle</u> is that issues of inequity of the bail determination or in the establishment of the right to equal treatment as an individual were not limited to those who were financially poor. These issues extended beyond the simplicity of wealth and poverty, but have found their locus in the cost of equal treatment. Equality before the law should know no economic distinction. This book will delineate: first, that economic distinctions do apply, and that they need not be the sole criteria for the application of equal justice. Second, that other criteria do exist which can be used in the determination of release pending trial aside from those which are financial.

A SOCIOLOGICAL ANALYSIS OF BAIL

To examine coherently the complexities of the bail phenomenon, it is important that a consistent frame of reference be provided for such an examination. First, a look at the sociology of jurisprudence will set the stage for an analysis of the sociolegal aspects of specific bail action. Second, the bail action will be surveyed to see if it applies consistently the theory as it has been presented. These issues will be put in a framework of the modern legal theory of Roscoe Pound and the analysis of Pound's theory and its updating by Richard Quinney. These men have written on sociological jurisprudence and the theory of interests. Their analyses of interests in conflict offer a modern format for examination of ancient adversarial procedure in its current context. While these authors do not make a direct correlation between ancient adversarial procedure and the modern, in this chapter these correlations will be highlighted.

Roscoe Pound who founded and developed the American "school of sociological jurisprudence," offers an interesting frame of reference for research into sociological and legal questions. He sought to bring social reality and legal processes into closer harmony, and in the process of so doing began to construct a sociological jurisprudence. The starting point of sociological jurisprudence was the concept of social control: "The pressure upon each man brought to bear by his fellow men in order to constrain him to do his part in upholding civilized society and to deter him from anti-social conduct, that is, conduct at variance with the postulates of the social order."[63] As Geis points out,

> Without organized social control, man's aggressive self-assertion would prevail over his cooperative social tendency and civilization would come to an end. Pound could only agree with Aristotle's belief that man is inherently the fiercest of beasts. Law was seen as a highly specialized form of social control whose purpose was 'social engineering,' the adjusting of relationships to meet prevailing ideas of fair play. Other segments of the network of social control - such as morals, religion, and education - interact with law to regulate human behavior in varying combinations of strength, depending upon the temper of different kinds of societies in different historical epochs.[64]

A theory of interests is central to sociological jurisprudence. An interest is defined by Pound as a "claim, a want, a demand of a human being or group of human beings which the human being or group of human beings seeks to satisfy and of which social engineering in a civilized society must take account."[65] Pound relies almost exclusively on the assertions that persons make in legal proceedings and press in legislative proposals as true indicators of their interest vis-a-vis the legal system.

Pound rates these claims according to their social intensity. First is the social interest in general security against those forms of action that threaten the social group; second is the social interest in security of social institutions; third is the general interest in morals; forth, the social interest in the conservation of resources; fifth, the social interest in general progress involving the development of human powers and of human control over nature for the satisfaction of human wants; sixth is the social interest in the individual life, which includes physical, mental and economic life as well as freedom of self-assertion. The early sociological roots of Pound's jurisprudential theory are found in the writings of Edward A. Ross,[66] Albion W. Small,[67] and Lester F. Ward.[68] These American sociologists have left a legacy in law. From Edward A. Ross, Pound drew his definition and theory of social control. From Albion W. Small, Pound developed his understanding of interests. And from Lester F. Ward, Pound devised an organic model for the understanding of the law and its relationship to the social structure.[69] It is important to note that at this point in an understanding of the relationship of Pound's theory to bail, we must look at the particular social interests which come into play in the bail setting. These social interests are Pound's first social interest - general security against those forms of action that threaten the social group - and Pound's sixth interest - in the individual life, which includes physical, mental and economic life as well as freedom of self-assertion. These two relationships - the individual and the general security of the group - are mediated in a courtroom, especially by interests such as the social interest in the security of institutions, namely the court of law, and third, in Pound's schema, the general interest in morals. These are the particular aspects of Pound's interest structure that we find at work in the bail setting process at arraignment in Criminal Court.

It is important to recognize that the theory of interest as enunciated in Pound's sociological jurisprudence is only an approach to a practical evaluation of legislative and judicial decisions. Decisions in criminal court particularly are not based on precedent or antecedent, if you will, but anticipated social consequences. Law in this sense, according to Pound, is to adjust social conflict. Any casual observation of the arraignment proceeding and the setting of bail in the criminal court will make this contention clear.[70]

While sociological jurisprudence sees law as an instrument which controls interests according to the requirements of the social order, a sociological theory of interests is a substantive evolution from Pound's initial formulation. The sociological theory of interest differs from Pound's formulation in that it builds upon a conflict model of society and postulates that law is representative of particular interests rather than of society as a whole. This is a dramatic shift from Pound's concept of law as the arbiter or

21

adjustor of social conflict. Here we find in this
particular view a vision of law as the product of different groups in a struggle to make their particular
interests established. This relationship of law and
particular interests is found discussed in the writings
of Max Weber,[71] Talcott Parsons,[72] and C. Wright
Mills.[73] In the sociological theory of interests,
society, primarily is characterized "by diversity,
conflict, coercion, and change, rather than consensus
and stability."[74] Unlike Ward and Small, who opted for
an equilibrium model of harmonious and regulated
evolutionary growth, this theory is much closer to
Dahrendorf's conflict model of society.[75] He postulates
that all units of social organization are continuously
changing unless some force intervenes to arrest this
change. Where there is social life there is conflict
rather than static equilibrium. In this model a key
factor is the notion of constraint. Social organizations are held together by constraint, not consensus.
As conflict generates change, so constraint is seen to
generate conflict.

This theoretical approach expresses the movement
away from justice as a balancing of the scales to a
new search for power in the adjudicate of and satisfaction of interests. It reflects the growing power
and presence of what we have come to colloquially know
as interest groups in the society. We find the courts
responding to the pressure of interest groups. Among
interest groups that work on behalf of the defendant
in the criminal court arraignment and bail proceeding
we find such organizations as the Legal Aid Society,[76]
the Vera Institute of Justice,[77] Bail Out,[78] the
Women's Bail Fund.[79] This brings us to the consideration of the social implications of bail in the contemporary American scene. Law is seen as the result of
the operation of interests, the instrument which
functions outside of particular interests; though law
may operate to control interests, it is in the first
place created by interests. The former President of
the United States, Lyndon Baines Johnson, illustrated
this premise when he signed the Bail Reform Act of 1966
on June 22 that year. At that time he said, "This
legislation, for the first time requires that the decision to release a man prior to trial be based on facts
- like community and family ties and past record. In
the words of this act, 'a man, regardless of his
financial status - shall not needlessly be detained
. . .when detention serves neither the ends of justice
nor the public interest.'"[80]

Law is seldom the product of the whole society.
Law incorporates the interests of specific persons and
groups in society rather than representing the interests
of all the members of the society as such. Law consists of the interests of only specific segments of the
population. Law is made by men, particularly men
representing special interests, who have the power to
translate their interests into public policy. In
opposition to the pluralistic conception of politics,
law does not represent the compromise of the diverse
interests of society, but supports some interests at
the expense of others. The relationship between bail
and detention is reflective of this type of supporting
position.

> When the activities of . . .criminals
> become the subject of public discussion
> or when the specific crime committed by
> one of them enrages the community, the
> community tends to label the alleged
> offender as dangerous and the judge often
> reflects this view in his use of bail to
> maintain the alleged offender in custody.
> In our large cities. . .public pressure
> does not develop in many aggravated cases
> in which the police feel that the public
> interest would be better served were the
> alleged offender detained.[81]

Here interests are at work. They do not always manifest themselves in the manner which some groups such as
the police would prefer. However, it is this very
definite lack of interest or difference in the direction
of expression of interest which allows for the conflic-
tual dimension of interest resolution to emerge.

There are four propositions characterizing the
sociological approach to a theory of interests. First,
law is the creation and interpretation of specialized
rules in a politically organized society. There are
authority relationships in all social groupings. These
can be both formal and informal. These authority
formulations cut across all areas of life and serve as
a control system. They provide means for assuring
compliance with the rules which are prescribed, or the
conduct which is proscribed. Such systems may rely on
formal sanctions.

The legal system is the most explicit form of
social control. The laws consist of 1) specific rules

23

of conduct; 2) planned use of sanctions; 3) designated officials to interpret and enforce the rules. As society becomes increasingly complex, law becomes more important as the system of social control. Law means authorized power to govern lives and activities of individuals and roots in the territorial organization, the state. Systems of law are the specialized rule systems of politically organized societies.

Law is more than an abstract system of rules. It is a special kind of institution in society. Law is an integral part of the society, not solely autonomous and developing according to its own internal logic. Although it has happened that law can develop apart from its social context. Even in this case it becomes then challenged by groups representing interests which they feel are not met by the autonomy or internal logic of the legal system. The law operates as a social force and thus as a social product. Law is not only statutes, briefs and opinions, but also a method or a process of doing something. As such, law is dynamic and a force in that it is continually being created and interpreted. Law in action involves the making of specialized legal decisions by various authorized agents. In organized society human actions are regulated by those invested with the authority to make these decisions in society's name. In the criminal court system the decision is made by the judge. He is helped in the process by a variety of ancillary agents who comprise the system we call the administration of justice. Law is thus an aspect of public policy and administered to govern the lives and activities of the inhabitants of a given society. As such it does not and cannot represent the norms and values of all persons in a society. Whenever the law is created or interpreted, some values are assured and others are negated or ignored. The political nature of law is basic to the sociological theory of interest.

All organized societies adjudicate interests. The governing process in politically organized society operates according to the interests that characterize sociologically differentiated positions. Since various kinds of interests are distributed among the positions and because the positions are differently equipped with the ability to command, public policy represents certain interests in society. Politically organized society may be viewed as a differentiated interest structure.

Each segment of society has its own values, norms

24

and ideological orientations. When these concerns are considered important for the existence and welfare of their respective positions, they may be defined as interests. Interests can be categorized according to the ways in which activities are generally pursued in a society; that is, according to the institutional orders of society. Interests, then, are the institutional concerns of the segments of society. Thus, interests are grounded in the segments of society and represent the institutional concerns of these segments.

These institutional orders include the political, the social, the economic, the familial and the educational. Our concern is with law in the social order. The segments of society differ in the extent to which their interests are organized. The segments themselves are broad statistical aggregates containing persons of similar age, sex, class, status, occupation, race, ethnicity and religion, for example. All these segments have formal interests, that is, the interests are advantageous to the segment which are not consciously held by the incumbents and are not organized for action. Active interests are those that are manifest to persons in the segments and are sufficiently organized to serve as the basis for representation in policy decisions. Groups organize to promote their interests and their purposes. They are interest groups which form within the broad spectrum of society to foster their interests. Public policy for this heterogeneous society is the result of the successful fostering of these interest groups. We shall see how these interests are manifested in the interaction in the courtroom.

Finally, the interest structure of an organized society is characterized by unequal distribution of power and conflict. Basic to the interest structure is the concept that power is unevenly distributed among interest groups. These diverse interests therefore are constantly struggling to turn their interests into an expression of power. This expression of power is manifest as public policy. Power as the ability to shape public policy produces conflicts between competing segments.[82] Conflict produces in its turn differential distribution of power. Coherence in the interest structure is thus assured by the exercise of force and constraint by the conflicting segments of the interest structure. This is very clearly seen in the bail phenomenon as an instrument of social control for those who are accused of an alleged crime and who may be released pending trial. In the conflict-power model

25

of interest structure, organized society is held together by these conflicting elements and functions
being regulated by other elements in the society.

The law is formulated and administered within the
interest structure of a politically organized society.
It is formulated and administered by the segments of
society able to incorporate their interests into the
creation and interpretation of public policy. Rather
than representing the institutional concerns of all
segments of society, law secures the interests of
particular segments. Law supports one point of view
at a time.

The content of law, which includes substantive
regulations and procedural rules, represents the
interests of segments of society that have the power
to shape public policy. Formulation of law allows some
segments of society to protect and foster their own
interests. By formulating law, some segments are able
to control others to their own advantage. Since legal
formulations do not provide specific instructions for
interpreting law, administration of law is largely a
matter of discretion on the part of legal agents.
Latitude in interpretation of statutory law is left to
judicial discretion. The decisions which are reached
tend to support the interests of some segments of
society while impeding others. This places the pursuit
of particular interests in adversarial context. The
interest structure of organized society is responsible
for the general design of the administration of justice.

Since law is formulated and administered within
the interest structure of politically organized
society, it follows that law changes with modifications
in that structure. New and shifting demands require
new laws. When the interests that underlie a law are
no longer relevant to groups in power, the law will be
reinterpreted or changed to incorporate the dominant
interests. When Caleb Foote initiated his study of
"The Administration of Bail in New York City,"[83] in
1958, it was a struggle to find even initial funds to
commence the project which was nearly scrapped.[84]
Within eight years international conferences were
being held on the issue of bail in the United States
and in England. The decade of the 1960s has provided
the groundwork for bail reevaluation. The sociological
theory of interests thus revolves around the theme of
interest conflicts and power.

No real understanding of legal phenomena can be achieved if the power dimension is ignored. An analysis of law in terms of its functions tends to take stability as its point of departure. This has been extensively criticized by Dahrendorf,[85] Bierstedt[86] and Quinney.[87] The approach taken by them sees equilibrium as a momentary by-product of a constant quest for power by different groups. The legal system incorporates power in at least two ways. First, the makers, interpreters, administrators and enforcers of law themselves hold positions of considerable power. The legal functionary is constrained by role definition, by ideals of justice and practical limitations. The second power aspect of the legal system lies in its elaboration of the rights and duties accruing to the various constituent social elements. The claim to rights is usually accompanied by some show of support. The legal recognition of rights implies power to enforce such rights through legal institutions. The entire movement of bail reform has been to foster the recognition of the right to bail. Such awareness of the constitutional and statutory nature of the right enabled those who previously had been less aware or unaware of that right to seek it. The majority of the defendants in the criminal court system, for a variety of reasons, either did not know the options they were entitled to or else did not know how to exercise those options.[88] While the Constitution demands that one be advised of rights, the one who is advised can lack the instrumentality for obtaining those rights.

It is in the formal organization of associations that social power is transformed into interest groups which possess a certain amount of informal authority in the community. When social action and interaction proceed wholly in conformity to the norms of the formal organizations in society, power is dissolved without residue into authority. This is a type of cooptation. The right to force is, however, attached to certain statuses within the social aggregate, and this constitutes a unique type of formal authority. It is by authority in an association that persons exercise control over fellow members. Power in these cases is attached to statuses, not to persons, and is wholly institutionalized as authority. Thus we see in the criminal court status activity and role performance. Social action does not proceed in precise or absolute conformity to the norms of formal organization. Power spills over the status holders, who only imperfectly contain power in its expression as authority. That spillage, if you will, is absorbed by informal organizations where the prestige of the particular status gives way to the esteem for persons who are searching for status, and the social interaction of the members of that informal organization proceeds not only in terms of the explicit norms of the informal organization but in terms of the implicit extra-associational forms whose locus is in the community at large and which may or may not conflict at strategic points with the informal association's norms.

Power also exists in the community in an amorphous form. It resides in embryonic groups struggling for a hearing. Power emerges in this context in the relations of like or unlike groups. It may present itself in the context of the unorganized community with a formal institution. Such groups as the Women's Bail Fund and Bail Out are illustrations of the unorganized in the struggle for power. This power may also structure itself into a more defined organization such as the Vera Institute of Justice or the Legal Aid Society. The important point is that power arises only in social opposition of some kind. The bail situation is one such oppositional situation. Organizations which are not directly connected with the issue of bail have also taken on bail projects. This indicates not only their concern but a sense of an awareness of an unmet need or expression of power in the community.

Organizations may adapt to new interests or concentrate their resources on newly rediscovered interests because they have the components of successful power realization. These components are first, numbers of people; second, social organizations; third, resources. Power resides in the successful combination of these factors. Each factor alone or in combination with only one other is inadequate. All three must be present in concert. For example, to have an organization without funds will vitiate any potential that it may have. This has been the problem with the Women's Bail Fund, which lacked an organizational basis even though it had resources. It was unable to obtain release for women detained since it was not recognized as an approved agency for release. Its representatives have until recently not been members of the legal profession. They have therefore been unable to gain access to the women's detention facility. To have numbers and resources but lack organization will also preclude success. A group with adequate organization, even with limited resources and small numbers, will be more

28

powerful than one lacking the effective combination. It
is perhaps interesting to note at this point as we move
to a consideration of a particular challenge to the bail
phenomenon how traditionally power has been equated with
wealth or money in our society. The thrust of this book
is to show that this has been too narrow a focus. This
one dimension of resources in the Bierstedt analogy
lacks balance because it does not possess the combination of organization and numbers. Our society has
placed the emphasis on wealth as the instrumentality
of assessing the willingness of a party to exercise
responsible citizenship or responsible membership in
the social community, to accept social control. When
the economic premises underlying that assumption of
responsibility come into question or are rejected, the
narrowness of that particular base will become clear.
This understanding of the tripartite nature of power
helps us to understand how at the present time there
are increasing numbers of social groups forming and
growing whose purposes are to enlist membership and to
organize resources in order to effectuate change in the
manner in which bail as a social process is administered. It also clearly illustrates how the economic factor
is only one factor among the three power dimensions,
and while it has appeared as central this is because
the other aspects have been neglected.

A legal challenge to the bail system and its social implications

The Legal Aid Society is one organization which
has arisen to protect the rights of the individual in
the criminal justice system which has been, as we have
seen, highly bureaucratized. The Legal Aid Society had
initiated a suit challenging the entire bail system on
the question of its legality. It rested its argument
squarely on the law but it delineated more than just
the legal aspects of the problem, but the additional
social aspects of the problem.

> The inescapable conclusion is that the fact
> of detention itself causes those detained
> to be convicted far more often and sentenced
> much more severely than those who are re-
> leased. . .the present bail system creates
> two classes of accused distinguished by their
> wealth or lack of it: those who are released
> are relatively more likely to have a favorable
> outcome in their cases, and those who are
> detained in lieu of bail and therefore much

more likely to be convicted and get a
prison sentence.[89]

This same comment has been raised by earlier studies,
those of Rankin,[90] Wald,[91] and Sturz.[92] Until now no
one has examined precisely the relationship socially or
legally between the process of bail and the outcome
based on a thorough examination of individual cases.
This book attempts to provide the sociological case
analysis. It is our suggestion that the Legal Aid study
which paralleled this book provided the first comprehensive legal challenge to the entire bail process.

The bail system as it now operates under the control of the administration of the criminal justice
system, created two classes of defendants. These are
those who are detained and those who are released prior
to trial. The difference in outcome depends on whether
the accused does or does not have resources to obtain
his freedom before trial. In this way the present
system operates to deny the defendant the equal protection of the law in violation of the 14th Amendment to
the United States Constitution, and Article I Section
5 of the New York State Constitution.

The purpose of the equal protection clause of the
14th Amendment is "that all persons in similar circumstances shall be treated alike."[93] A statutory scheme
which on its face need not be considered discriminatory
nonetheless violates the equal protection clause where
it has come to be applied in such a way that only one
class of people suffer under that system.[94] It is
essential to remember that the Constitution permits
qualitative differences only[95] in terms of the Legal
Aid study. There are differences in outcome between
those detained and those released, and these differences are not caused by any per se "qualitative
differences" between the two groups of cases. "Qualitative" differences, such as type and seriousness of
charge, weight of evidence, aggravation of circumstances, nature of prior criminal record and background
were shown not to be the reason for differing treatment.
Detention in lieu of bail turns on the issue of wealth
alone, and the amount of money the accused has is not
a qualitative basis for treating him differently from
other persons similar to him in all other respects.

The Supreme Court in <u>Williams</u> vs. <u>Illinois</u> calls
attention to "the need to be open to reassessment of
ancient practices other than those explicitly mandated

by the Constitution. . . . [96] A need which is especially important in a situation such as the present one.
It has also been shown how these ancient practices over
the years have led to a system which treats some people
more harshly than others only because they do not have
a predetermined amount of money to obtain their liberty.

Judge Skelly Wright has observed in a landmark
opinion, whenever a "critical personal right" is infringed by an existing legal classification, that
classification must be subjected to "the gauntlet of
judicial review searching for an adequate justification."[97]

The explanation for. . .judicial scrutiny
of practices which, although not directly
discriminatory, nevertheless fall harshly
on such groups relates to the judicial
attitude toward legislative and administrative judgments. Judicial deference to
these judgements is predicated in the
confidence courts have that they are just
resolutions of conflicting interests.
This confidence is often misplaced when
the vital interests of the poor and of
racial minorities are involved.[98]

Two recent Supreme Court decisions which have
clear ramification for the present bail system are
Williams vs. Illinois and Tate vs. Short.[99] In
Williams, the Court held that a frequently used manner
of sentencing an accused is to pay a fine or to work
it off in jail at the conclusion of his jail term; this
denied to an indigent the equal protection of the law.
The fact that the mode of sentencing which was invalidated was both venerable and non-discriminatory on
its face did not rescue it in the Court's view. Whatever valid justifications there may be for imprisoning
a convicted person, the inability to raise a certain
amount of money is not among them.[100] Consequently
in Tate, the Court later held that to imprison an
indigent for non-payment of a fine which had been
imposed in lieu of a jail sentence was likewise a
violation of the equal protection clause. It was
found to be "unconstitutional discrimination" because
"petitioner was subject to imprisonment solely because
of indigency."[101] The present New York bail system
creates a dichotomy in the treatment of persons accused
of a crime which is discriminatory as any scheme yet
invalidated by the courts of this country under the
equal protection clause. The decision for allowing

release on bail is not based on consistently applied,
rationally determined procedure. The application of
the rules of bail has been based not on all of the
required criteria but on selected application of some
criteria. In the criminal justice system in New York
County there is one issue which above all determines
the outcome of the case: was the accused released or
detained while awaiting disposition of the charges
against him? This was central in the Legal Aid study.
The correlation between the outcome and detention of
the defendant becomes a major social factor extending
well beyond the application of the rules of justice in
the criminal justice system. It affects the personal
life and the social future of an individual who may be
justly or unjustly afflicted with a criminal record of
arrest or conviction. Dispositions which are based on
incomplete application of the criteria as required by
the law are a denial of the equal protection of the
laws.

In Chapter II the initial social setting of the
arraignment proceeding in the criminal court in New
York County will be described. Suffice it to note the
bustle of activity, the congestion, the number of cases
to be heard, to understand that the time available to
the investigation of the individual circumstances of
each defendant is severely limited. Yet, in that courtroom a decision of tremendous importance, whether the
State will deprive a man of his liberty before it has
proved it has a right to do so, is reached in an
instant.

> Arraignment proceedings are handled at
> breakneck speed with arraigning judge
> arriving at his decision on bail within
> seconds. . .in the vast majority of cases,
> the judge simply announces a sum and
> proceeds to the next case.[102]

Chapter II will show how this decision has been arrived
at. The direct purpose of this book is not to establish
a correlation between the pretrial disposition of the
defendant and the outcome of his particular case. It
is to examine the process itself and the manner in
which the criteria by which the process is activated
is utilized. However, as the Legal Aid Society study
showed, the outcome of this bail setting process is
determinant of the future of these individuals within
the criminal justice system's context. Undoubtedly the
wider social ramifications of such activity demand the

kind of careful analysis of cases that we have hoped to present. As the Legal Aid study has said:

> Nonetheless, even though what has been documented mathematically, that is, that the bail or release question is outcome determinative, it is also generally accepted as true, the process by which this crucial decision is reached is shockingly barren of basic guarantees for the accused. This lack of fundamental procedural safeguards violates the due process clauses of the 14th Amendment to the Constitution of the United States and Article I, Section 6 of the Constitution of the State of New York.[103]

Due process of law is not a rigid or static expression. It is a concept of what is just, fair and right.[104] The extent to which procedural due process must be afforded is determined by considering "the extent to which defendants may be 'condemned to suffer grievous loss'" and weighing "whether /their/ interest in avoiding that loss outweighs the governmental interest in summary ajudication."[105]

As to the first branch of that inquiry, the extent of the plaintiff's losses is clear. In New York County in 1969, according to the Department of Correction statistics, 38,771 people were remanded in lieu of bail. In the Annual Report of the New York City Department of Correction[106] these figures appear. Such incarceration entails many obvious losses. A man in prison in lieu of bail loses his liberty. His family is disrupted. He is deprived of any meaningful contact with other human beings, especially his family. His income and possibly his job are lost, which in turn causes additional hardships on those dependent on him. He is forced to survive at the most minimal level of human existence, and is subjected to overcrowding, inadequate food, sexual assaults and frequent acts of violence. He is exposed to people with a wide range of criminal experience and is housed with people suffering from mental illness, addiction or narcosis. The pressures of this type of existence have caused the number of suicides and suicide attempts in the New York jails to mount steadly in recent years.[107]

Incarcerated persons suffer further loss with

respect to outcome of their cases. They are hampered in
the preparation of defense. They are denied the chance
to demonstrate rehabilitation. They are impeded in
consultation with counsel. It has been shown that all
other things being equal, they are convicted more often,
given prison terms more often, and more often received
harsher sentences.

With regard to the other branch of the test
enunciated, namely "the governmental interest in summary
adjudication," one word sums up that interest: money.
There is no legitimate interest other than the alloca-
tion elsewhere of its resources for the State of New
York to allow the bail setting process to continue to be
deficient in its application of the presumption of
innocence and of due process of law. The bail decision
is an extremely critical stage of any criminal proceeding. It has been shown that in many cases it is the
ultimate constitutional right to liberty which is at
stake when a judge issues an order for detention. It
is not a sufficient answer to say that there is not
enough money available to grant procedural due
process.[108]

Therefore the Legal Aid study suggested in its
challenge to the courts the following constitutional
requisites for any hearing at which bail may be set.
First, in every instance where the issue arises the
court must assume that the accused is entitled to pretrial release. The American Bar Association stated
unequivocally that "it should be presumed that the
defendant is entitled to be released on order to
appear, or on his own recognizance."[109] The Bar
Association report continues:

> The law favors the release of defendants
> pending determination of guilt or inno-
> cence. Deprivation of liberty pending
> trial is harsh and oppressive in that it
> subjects persons whose guilt has not been
> judicially established to economic and
> psychological hardships, interferes with
> their ability to defend themselves, and in
> many cases deprives their families of
> support. Moreover, the maintenance of
> jailed defendants and their families
> represents a major public expense.[110]

The evidence clearly indicates that the error rate
among detained persons is very high. In other words,

of the people who are detained awaiting disposition of their case, many are ultimately convicted but get no prison term, or else have their cases dismissed. Thus, the present bail system is not consistent with the presumption of innocence by punishing large numbers of people whose guilt the State is unable to prove. Further, half of all the people who secure pretrial release are ultimately not convicted.[111] Under these circumstances, presumption of innocence must be regarded as more than abstract principle. It further demands that the accused be released pending trial.

The only legitimate interest that the State can have in placing restriction on an accused's right to liberty is the reasonable assurance that he will continue to appear in court.[112] Without a showing that restrictions on an accused's liberty are necessary to assure his reappearance, such restrictions violate the constitutional guarantees of due process and equal protection.

Second, despite the presumption of the accused's innocence, and not withstanding the likelihood in many cases that measures short of requiring a bail bond would be reasonable, the district attorney does not recommend and justices do not consider or impose non-financial alternatives to bail. This book will point to the small percentage of cases in which non-financial alternatives to bail have been employed. Even if the accused has no roots in the community and no close family ties that would reasonably assure his appearance in court when required, the bail setting court must attempt to fashion non-financial conditions of release.[113] It has been held in similar contexts that before a trial judge may confine a person in custody, he must find and utilize the least burdensome alternative that would serve the purpose of confinement. Applying "the principle of least restrictive alternative" to a situation directly analogous to bail setting procedures, the court in Covington vs. Harris[114] held that before a trial court can order a civil commitment of a person to a mental institution it must satisfy itself that no less onerous disposition would serve the purpose of commitment.[115] The Supreme Court has long held that where the fundamental personal liberties are involved, government must pursue its legitimate interest by the least restrictive means possible.[116] The non-financial conditions of release which the district attorney must investigate and wherever possible recommend, and which the justices and judges must require whenever possible, would include a) releasing the accused into the care of a person or organization responsible for assuring his continued appearance in court;[117] b) placing reasonable restrictions on the accused's activities, associations, movement or residence;[118] c) permitting daytime release or imposing other conditions requiring the accused to return to custody on weekends or at specified hours.[119]

The American Bar Association project on minimum standards for criminal justice, the National Conference on Bail and Criminal Justice, and legal commentators urge such use of non-financial conditions of release rather than the automatic imposition of bail. This chapter establishes that bail in its historical and its social inception was not a financial obligation essentially. In an article in the Yale Law Journal the situation has been presented.

> If the accused is unable to provide security because he has no assets, other restrictions must be considered if imposition of bail is not to be used as a subterfuge for denial of release. These might include release in custody of a third party, such as the accused's employer, minister, attorney or a private organization; release subject to a duty to report periodically to the court or other public official, or even released subject to a duty to return to jail each night. Admittedly the setting of individualized conditions poses a more difficult problem than the automatic imposition of bail. Yet if the risk of flight is not so great as to justify total subordination of the presumption of innocence, an attempt to find such conditions must be made.[120]

The use of non-financial conditions of release would bring the law more nearly in line with the presumption of innocence; it would end the present constitutionally impermissible system of making an accused's pretrial release dependent solely on his ability to pay for it; would end much of the de facto preventive detention of the poor; and would provide greater assurance of the accused's appearance than does the bail bond.

What is essential to note in the Legal Aid Society's brief to the court is that while the citations and argument were couched in terms of the law and previous decisions, the issues which are at stake extend well beyond an issue of legality. They include the well-being of the individual in the society at large. We can see in this determination the role in which interests play. We see in the presentation of the Legal Aid Society's brief to the court an organization's attempt to coalesce and to present a powerful argument for the change of circumstances which are contrary to the interests of a significant population in our society.

FOOTNOTES

1. Elsa de Hass, Antiquities of Bail Origin and Development in Criminal Cases to the Year 1275. New York: Columbia University Press, 1940.

2. Emile Durkheim, The Division of Labor in Society. New York: The Free Press, 1947.

3. Benjamin Nelson, "Sciences and Civilization, 'East' and 'West.'" Boston Studies with Philosophy of Science, R.S. Cohen and M.W. Wartofsky, eds. Vol. xi, 1974, pp. 459-63.

4. H. Bracton, On the Laws and Customs of England, translated and edited by Samuel H. Thorne. Cambridge: Harvard University Press, 1968, II, 345, 371.

5. Henry S. Maine, Ancient Law. London: J. Murray, 1863, ch. 1.

6. Paul Vinogradoff, Outlines of Historical Jurisprudence. London: 1920-22, I, p. 312.

7. William A. Morris, The Frankpledge System. Cambridge, 1910, in Harvard Historical Studies, Vol. xiv, p. 155.

8. Otto Von Gierke, Deutsches Privatrecht. Leipsig, 1895, Vol. iii, p. 524 (1917). See also Andre Fliniaux, Le Vadimonium. Paris: Rousscau, 1908, ch. 5.

9. De Haas, op cit., p. 33, note 10.

10. Pipe Rolls "Pipe Roll Society Publications," 6-10 Henry II (1159-64). London, 1884-1925.

11. Morton W. Bloomfield, "Beowulf, Byrhtmoth, and the Judgment of God: Trial by Combat in Anglo-Saxon England." Speculum, Vol. XLIV, #4 (October 1969), pp. 549-549.

12. "Sir Launfal" in Middle English Verse Romances. Donald B. Sands, ed. New York: Holt, Rinehart & Winston, Inc., 1966, pp. 216-217, 11. 430-500.

13. Sir F. Pollock and F.W. Maitland, The History of English Law Before the Time of Edward I, Second Edition. London: 1898, Vol. II, p. 584f.

14. Thomas A. Green, "Societal Concepts of Criminal Liability for Homicide in Medieval England." Speculum, Vol. XLVII, #4, (October 1972), p. 671.

15. Sir Edward Coke, A Little Treatise of Baile and Maineprize. London: William Cooke, 1637 (2nd ed.), Chapter Two.

16. D.M. Stenton (ed.), Rolls of the Justices in Eyre, Being Rolls of Pleas and Assizes for Lincolnshire 1218-19 and Worcestershire, 1221. London: 1934, pp. xiviii-lxxi.

17. Bloomfield, op. cit., pp. 551-552.

18. H.G. Richardson and G.O. Sayles, The Governance of of Medieval England from the Conquest to Magna Carta. Chicago: Aldine Publishing Co., 1963, pp. 195-196.

19. The raising of the "hue and cry" on discovery of a crime and "outlawry" or the "wolf's head" which allowed the miscreant to be killed on sight are illustrative. Also the communities were close knit and the presence of strangers was a source of suspicion. See Chambliss, "A Sociological Analysis of the Law of Vagrancy" in Quinney, ed., Crime and Justice in Society, pp. 55-68.

20. Green, op. cit., p. 670.

21. Elsa De Hass, Antiquities of Bail; Origins and Historical Development in Criminal Cases to the Year 1275. New York: Columbia University Press, 1940, p. 40.

22. "Gamelyn" in Sands (ed.) op. cit., p. 168, 11, 440-443.

23. 3 Edward I, c 15 Statute of Westminister I, 1275.

24. De Haas, op. cit., p. 57.

25. Bracton, On the Laws and Customs of England, Samuel Thorne, ed. Cambridge: The Harvard University Press, 1968, Vol. II, p. 375.

26. "Magna Carta," in Milton Viorst, <u>The Great Documents of Western Civilization</u>. New York: Chilton Books, 1965, pp. 113-47.

27. "The Habeas Corpus Act of 1679," in Viorst <u>vide supra</u>.

28. "The Bill of Rights of 1689," in Viorst <u>vide supra</u>.

29. "The Bill of Rights of 1689," <u>loc. cit.</u>

30. Sir Edward Coke, <u>A Little Treatise of Baile and Maineprize</u>. London: W. Cooke, 1637 (2nd ed.).

31. Ronald Goldfarb, <u>Ransom: A Critique of the American Bail System</u>. New York: Harper and Row, 1965, Chapter I.

32. Bernard Botein, "The Manhattan Bail Project: Its Impact on Criminology and the Criminal Law Process," <u>Texas Law Review</u>, February 1965, p. 319.

33. "Borg," pledge or caution money.

34. "Borwe," dative of "borge." See F.H. Stratmann, <u>Middle English Dictionary</u>, Oxford: Modern Edition Reprints, 1958 (original 1891).

35. "Gamelyn," in <u>Middle English Verse Romances</u>, Sands, ed., pp. 154-181.

36. "Gamelyn," p. 168, 1. 441.

37. "Gamelyn," p. 176, 11. 735-752.

38. "Gamelyn," p. 178, ;;. 795-796.

39. Arthur L. Beeley, <u>The Bail System in Chicago</u>. 1927) Chicago: The University of Chicago Press, 1965 ed., especially Chapter One.

40. Ares, Rankin and Sturz, "The Manhattan Bail Project - An Interim Report on the Use of Pre-Trial Parole." 38 <u>New York University Law Review</u>, 67, 1963, pp. 70-71. See also <u>The 1972 Criminal Justice Plan</u>, New York: Executive Committee of the Criminal Justice Coordinating Council, 1972, p. 73. <u>John Bellamy et al</u> v. <u>The Judges</u>, Plaintiffs' Memorandum in New York Supreme Court Appellate Division, First Department. New York: The Legal Aid Society, March 1972, p. 3.

41. Bellamy v. Judges, pp. 27-28. Hereinafter cited as Legal Aid Study.

42. Legal Aid Study. "Conclusions." (G) p. 29. See also Abraham S. Blumberg, Criminal Justice, Chicago: Quadrangle Books, 1968, and the Criminal Court: An Organizational Analysis, New York: New School for Social Research doctoral dissertation, 1965, p. 310.

43. The 1972 Criminal Justice Plan, p. 73, and Sam J. Ervin, Jr., "Preventive Detention: An Empricial Analysis." Harvard Civil Rights Civil Liberties Law Review, Vol. VI #3, March 1971, pp. 291ff.

44. Stack v. Boyle 342 U.S. 1, 1951, pp. 7-8 (concurring opinion). Lockhart, Kamisar and Choper, American Constitutional Rights and Liberties. St. Paul: West Publishing Col, 1979, pp. 399-400.

45. Caleb Foote, "The Coming Constitutional Crisis in Bail" I 113, University of Pennsylvania Law Review, 1965, pp. 959-65.

46. "Magna Carta," vide supra, note 26.

47. Foote, "The Coming Constitutional Crisis. . . ." II, p. 966.

48. Charles Baron de Secondat Montesquieu, The Spirit of the Laws. New York: Hafner Publishing Co., 1949.

49. Foote, "The Coming Constitutional Crisis. . . ." II, p. 968.

50. "The Massachusetts Body of Liberties of 1641," in Annals of America, Vol. I, pp. 163-167. New York: Encyclopedia Britannica, 1968.

51. "An Ordinance for the Government of the Territory of the United States Northwest of the River Ohio," July 13, 1787, Article ii.

52. Judiciary Act of 1789, 1 Stat. 91, Sect. 33.

53. Bail and Summons: 1965. Proceedings of the National Conference on Criminal Justice. New York: The Vera Foundation, 1966. See last section.

54. United States v. Lawrence 26 Fed. Cas 887, 888
    (No. 15577) Circuit Court District of Columbia 1835.

55. Foote, "The Coming Constitutional Crisis. . . ."
    II, p. 993. See also United States v. Brawner,
    7 Fed. 86 (W.D. Tenn 1851); Harrison v. Stone 113
    Fla. 471, 152 So 19 (1934); United States v.
    Rumrich 180 F 2nd 575, 576 (2nd Circuit 1950).

56. Alexis de Tocqueville, Democracy in America, trans.
    G. Lawrence. New York: Anchor Books, 1969, pp.
    48-49.

57. Pound and Frankfurter (eds.), Criminal Justice
    in Cleveland. Cleveland: The Cleveland Foundation,
    1922, pp. 154-55, 184-187, 212-213, 290-292, 313-
    314.

58. "Freedom at a Price. Bailbondsmen Wield Surprising
    Power, Stir Growing Controversy." Wall Street
    Journal, Thursday, October 7, 1971, p. 1. See also
    Michael Pearl, "Hard Times on Bail Bond Row," New
    York, September 29, 1969, pp. 40-44.

59. "Hard Times on Bail Bond Row," p. 43, Table.

60. Stack v. Boyle, loc. cit.

61. Griffin v. Illinois 351 U.S. 12, 76 Supreme Court
    585. 1956. See also Draper v. Washington.

62. Nathan R. Sobel, The New Confession Standards
    Miranda v. Arizona. New York: Gould Publications,
    1966.

63. Roscoe Pound, Social Control Through Law. New
    Haven: Yale University Press, 1942.

64. Gilbert Geis, "Sociology and Sociological Juris-
    prudence: Admixture of Lore and Law." Kentucky
    Law Journal, Vol. 52 (Winter 1964), pp. 267-93.

65. Roscoe Pound, Jurisprudence. St. Paul: The West
    Publishing Col, 1959. Vol. III, The Scope and
    Subject Matter of Law, pp. 300-310.

66. Edward A. Ross, Social Control. New York:
    Macmillan Co., 1922.

67. Geis, op. cit., p. 283. See also Philip Selznick, "Legal Institutions and Social Control," Vanderbilt Law Review, Vol. 17, 1963.

68. Lester F. Ward, Applied Sociology. Boston: Ginn & Co., 1906. See also by the same author, Dynamic Sociology, New York: D. Appleton & Co., 1883.

69. Geis, op. cit., pp. 279-284.

70. Frederic Suffet, "Bail Setting: A Study of Courtroom Interaction," Crime and Delinquency, October 1966, p. 322.

71. Max Rheinstein, Max Weber on Law in Economy and Society. Cambridge: Harvard University Press, 1954, pp. 316-318.

72. Talcott Parsons, et. al, Theories of Society, Vol. I. New York: The Free Press, 1961.

73. C.W. Mills, "Structure of Power in American Society," British Journal of Sociology, Vol. 9, 1958, pp. 29-41.

74. Quinney, op. cit., p. 23.

75. Ralf Dahrendorf, "Out of Utopia: Toward a Reorientation in Sociological Analysis," American Journal of Sociology, Vol. 64, September 1958, pp. 115-127.

76. The Legal Aid Society Criminal Branch, 15 Park Row, New York City.

77. Vera Institute of Justice, 30 East 39th Street, New York City.

78. Bail Out! 235 West 28th Street, New York City. See also, "How the Church's Bail Fund Works," Central Journal, Central Presbyterian Church, Fall 1972, p. 9.

79. Women's Bail Fund, 475 Riverside Drive, New York City.

80. Lyndon B. Johnson address, June 22, 1966, upon signing of the Bail Reform Act of 1966, reported in Bail and Summons, p. xxxvi.

81. "Judge Supported on Prostitution," <u>New York Times</u>, August 1, 1971, p. 1.

82. Robert Bierstedt, "An Analysis of Social Power," <u>American Sociological Review</u>, Vol. 15, December 1950, p. 736.

83. Foote, "A Study of the Administration of Bail in New York City." 106 <u>University of Pennsylvania Law Review</u>, 1958, p. 693.

84. Foote, "Forward: Comment on the New York Bail Study." 106 <u>University of Pennsylvania Law Review</u>, 1958, p. 685.

85. Dahrendorf, <u>op. cit.</u>, p. 120.

86. Bierstedt, <u>op. cit.</u>, p. 736.

87. Quinney, <u>op. cit.</u>, p. 24.

88. Foote, "The Bail System and Equal Justice," <u>Federal Probation</u>, 23: September 1959, pp. 43-48. See also Langsdorff, "Is Bail a Rich Man's Privilege?" 7 <u>Federal Rules and Decisions</u>, pp. 309-310.

89. <u>Legal Aid Study</u>, p. 29.

90. Anne Rankin, "The Effect of Pre-Trial Detention," <u>New York University Law Review</u>, Vol. 39, June 1964, No. 4, pp. 641-645.

91. Patricia Wald, "Pretrial Detention and Ultimate Freedom," <u>New York University Law Review</u>, Vol. 39, June 1964, No. 4, pp. 633-635.

92. Ares, Rankin and Sturz, "The Manhattan Bail Project. . . ." p. 67. See also, "Wisconsin Bail Reform," <u>Wisconsin Law Review</u>, No. 2, 1971, pp. 594-604. In understanding the retributive nature of pretrial detention, George Herbert Mead's "The Psychology of Primitive Justice," <u>American Journal of Sociology</u>, Vol. 23, 1918, pp. 577-602, is helpful.

93. <u>F.S. Royster Guano Co.</u> v. <u>Virginia</u>, 253 U.S. 412, 415 (1920).

94. <u>Williams</u> v. <u>Illinois</u>, 399 U.S., 235, 242 (1970).

95. Legal Aid Study, p. 31.

96. Williams v. Illinois at 240.

97. Hobson v. Hanson, 269 Federal Supplement 401 (District of Columbia Circuit Court 1967).

98. Hobson v. Hanson at 507.

99. Tate v. Short, 401 U.S. 395 (1971).

100. Williams v. Illinois, 399 U.S. at 243.

101. Tate v. Short, 401 U.S. at 398.

102. Fabricant, "Bail as a Preferred Freedom and the Future of New York's Revision," 18 Buffalo Law Review, 303, 307 (1969).

103. Legal Aid Study, Chapter 2, Part E.

104. People v. Calozzo, 54 Misc. 2nd 687, 691, 283. N.Y.S. 2nd Department, 409, 415 (Supreme Court Kings County 1967).

105. Goldberg v. Kelly, 397 U.S. 254 - 263 (1970).

106. Annual Report, Department of Correction, New York County, 1969. Table 3.

107. Proposed Legislation and Recommendations of the Subcommittee on Penal and Judicial Reform of the Committee on Public Safety of the Council of the City of New York. Minutes, November 16, 1971, p. 576.

108. Millard v. Cameron, 373 F 2nd 468, 472, (D.C. Circuit 1966).

109. Standards Relating to Pre-Trial Release, American Bar Association Project on Minimum Standards For Criminal Justice, Washington, D.C., 1971.

110. Ibid., Part 1, Section 1.

111. Legal Aid Study, Table 4, p. 11.

112. People ex rel Lobell v. McDonnell, 296 N.Y. 109 (1947).

45

113. <u>U.S.</u> v. <u>Bronson</u>, 433 F 2nd 537 (D.C. Circuit 1970).

114. <u>Covington</u> v. <u>Harris</u>, 419 F 2nd 617, 623 (D.C. Circuit 1969).

115. <u>Hamilton</u> v. <u>Love</u>, 328 Fed. Supp. 1182, 1192-1193 (E.D. Arkansas 1971).

116. <u>Shelton</u> v. <u>Tucker</u>, 364 U.S. 479, 488 (1960).

117. <u>U.S.</u> v. <u>Bronson</u>, at 537.

118. <u>U.S.</u> v. <u>Alston</u>, 420 F 2nd 176 (D.C. Circuit 1969).

119. <u>U.S.</u> v. <u>Forrest</u>, 418 F 2nd 1186 (D.C. Circuit 1969).

120. "Bail: An Ancient Practice Reexamined," 70 <u>Yale Law Journal</u>, pp. 966, 975 (1961).

CHAPTER II

BAIL AS A SOCIAL PHENOMENON

Introduction

Since 1968, over 100,000 men and women over the
age of 16 have entered the halls of the Criminal
Court of the City of New York[1] each year to
take part in a social and legal process called arraignment because they have been arrested for an alleged
offense against the criminal code. Arraignment is the
process by which a person is brought before the court in
order to answer charges made against him in a formal
complaint, after receiving a copy of the complaint. To
these charges he may plead guilty or not guilty.[2]

One part of the arraignment proceeding for those
pleading not guilty is the setting of bail.

Every person accused of a crime is entitled to
apply for bail. Whether the application for bail will
be successful depends on the assessment of the court.
A sample of 878 cases from the files of the Legal Aid
Society in 1970, which were heard in Criminal Court of
the City of New York, will provide data for this
analysis of the bail setting procedure. The records of
the Legal Aid Society are chosen in preference to the
records which are kept in the Office of the Clerk of
the Court and in the Bureau of Statistics of the
Manhattan Criminal Court because they are kept in a
more precise chronological and detailed manner. These
cases are no longer pending; they are all closed.
These cases were among the last to be processed under
the Code of Criminal Procedure which was replaced by
the Criminal Procedure Law on September 1, 1971.[3]

Bail is that legal process whereby an agent of
the court, usually the judge, determines the right of
a person arrested on a criminal charge, the defendant,
to be released from custody pending trial on assurance
that he will subsequently appear for trial when
required.[4] The assurance may take the form of a
personal surety, that is, the accused with the consent
of the court will offer some pledge that he will
appear or the pledge is forfeit. Historically pledges
have been friends,[5] personal moneys, goods[6] or one's
word.[7] The bail bond has institutionalized these
arrangements.

The conditions of release, indicators of the
accused's reliability for appearance at trial, are
prior record, nature of offense, extent of evidence,
family ties, employment and residence.[8]

The Vera Institute of Justice[9] and the Legal Aid Society[10] have said that the bail determination at arraignment is the critical factor in the final disposition of each case since defendants unable to secure pretrial release have a higher rate of conviction and longer sentences to prison.

The decade of the 1960s has provided a climate for the reevaluation of bail, not paralleled by any other time in the history of bail in this country. The reasons for this are several. First, Supreme Court decisions have been rendered stipulating that the criminal court system has not upheld the rights of the accused.[11] These rights include the right to counsel,[12] the right to transcript,[13] the right to be advised of the prerogative of silence.[14] The impact of these individual cases became felt when the rules resulting from the Supreme Court precedents were applied to the lower courts. As pretrial and trial procedures were scrutinized more carefully, the logic of bail had to be brought into question. The first legal test of the bail system in the Criminal Court of the City of New York was Bellamy.[15]

Second, there are an increasing number of criminal cases whose defendants are incarcerated while awaiting prosecution. The attendant administrative problems of cost, care and feeding of defendants, overcrowding and lack of staff became evident.

The Senate Committee on Crime and Correction charged today that the New York City Department of Correction had made little or no effort to implement proposals it made after the October riots at the Tombs to humanize conditions there.

The committee accused the department of having a tendency to defend "its antiquated rules and procedures" and urged "a complete change of attitude" by department officials.

The committee said its proposals had called for "improved sanitary conditions, more humane and modern visiting procedures and methods for handling complaints, installation of telephones for use by inmates seeking to raise bail, methods of securing needed clothing for indigent inmates and better use of existing recreational facilities."

These suggestions are not complex; their implementation would cost little money, the committee said in a report to be released tomorrow.

Yet aside from some painfully slow progress on the telephone recommendation, there has been little or no effort to implement them.[16]

Third, the coverage increased on the issues of the criminal courts in the press and media as more of the people involved in the criminal justice system on a personal basis as defendants, complainants and their families publicized their problems.

In some cases, it was a delay caused by the courts or the jails or the police. In some, it was delay caused by the defendants themselves.

There were days when they came to court but their lawyers didn't. There were days when the Correction Department failed to bring them to court. There were medical exams ordered but never given, the transcripts ordered but never typed. There were months when the only entry in the court record was a hand-written note from the prisoner, asking for lower bail, or hearing or even a lawyer.[17]

Fourth, stories of people arrested, unable to make bail, held many months for trial, then acquitted or found to be victims of mistaken identity, raised the questions of innocence until proven guilty.

Haywood Boose was in cell D-3 on tier 5. He was awaiting trial on a burglary charge. He had been waiting 197 days.

Curtis Armstrong was down the aisle in cell C-6. In March the police had accused him of purse-snatching. It was 194 days later, and he was still to be tried.

Others on the tiers had waited longer: Jose Feliciano, eight months, sale of drugs; James Capers, 13-1/2 months, attempted murder. And George Colcloughley. He had been jailed in June of 1969 on a burglary charge; three months ago, after a year without a trial, he had asked a judge to either try him or dismiss the case. The judge declined both requests.[18]

The outbreak of rioting related to the multitudinous problems of the system brought a concentrated focus on the issues from officialdom.

The Board of Correction reported to Mayor Lindsay yesterday that a Young Lord who was found hanged in the Tombs last month was a suicide, the victim of an "inhuman" system of criminal justice and detention that "succeeded only in deranging him."

The Mayor had asked for a report from the board, an advisory group that he revived after the October prison riots, when the Young Lords charged that a member, Julio Roldan, had been murdered in the Manhattan House of Detention for Men.

The board's reply was a detailed account of the 33-year-old Puerto Rican radical's last days: His arrest under suspicious circumstances, his being insulted by the police, his arraignment before a harassed judge who heard 282 other cases that same day, his incarceration in a lonely maximum security part of the Tombs despite his increasing derangement, his cries through the night, his death.

Julio Roldan died by his own hand on Oct. 16, 1970, said William J. vanden Heuvel, the new chairman of the correction board, in his letter to Mr. Lindsay. But the intricate system of criminal justice which we have designed to protect the community and the individual succeeded only in deranging him and ultimately, instead of protecting him, it permitted his destruction.[19]

51

Federal[20] and State[21] legislation has resulted
from increased awareness of the problems attendant upon
bail.

Complexity of Bail Criteria

Until the beginning of the 1960s, the choice was
between bail bond or detention. The other forms of
pretrial release such as recognizance, cash bail,
realty bond or personal surety were unknown, unused or
unauthorized.[22] On September 1, 1971 the Code of
Criminal Procedure was replaced by the Criminal
Procedure Law. The new law allowed greater flexibility
in bail. Of the eight types of bail set forth in the
law release on recognizance, "ROR" and cash bail were
most frequently used primarily for minor crimes. Thus,
the accused's financial condition determined his
ability to obtain his status right. As Rankin,[23] Ares
and Sturz[24] have shown, this inability to post bail was
attended by problems such as difficulty in procuring
witnesses, preparing defense from detention, meeting
counsel, home problems attendant upon loss of job and/
or income, and disruption of family life. Also, the
accused held in detention entered the trial court in
custody and handcuffs, either in prison garb or in his
own clothes, and without the benefits available to the
bailed defendant who appeared for trial as a free man
entering with his counsel from the outside, and possibly without as many or none of the problems which
beset the detained accused. These perceived differences, though irrelevant to the issue before the court,
have had a bearing on the juries' decisions, according
to Patricia Wald.[25] They stigmatize the defendant by
creating, in the first instance, the appearance of a
convicted felon and in the second, a free man. Goffman
has demonstrated the significance of such stigmatization in our social relations.[26] Ironically, as the
decade of the '70s progressed bail fell into disuse as
plea negotiations rose in "respectability" and number.
The stigmatization remains.

What are the conditions which determine whether a
right to bail will be accorded and in what manner? The
State of New York's Code of Criminal Procedure specified
the conditions under which the accused may be admitted
to bail, but it carries the following note on the
amount:

Elements properly considered in fixing
the amount of bail are nature of
offense, penalty imposed, probability
of defendant's appearance or flight,
pecuniary and social condition, and
apparent nature and strength of proof
as bearing on the probability of his
conviction.[27]

Section 550, case note 4 states:

Amount of bail is a question of sound
discretion and judgment, depending upon
the primary conditions in the particular
case.[28]

These notes give no clue to a bail standard since no
instruction is given on how the various elements are
to be weighted vis-a vis one another, which conditions
are primary, and on the direction which bail is to vary
according to these elements. It does appear that the
amount of bail assessed is in direct relation to the
seriousness of the crime charged. This will be examined in Chapter V. Chapters III and IV will examine
the relationship of bail to the defendants' "pecuniary
and social condition."[29]

Pretrial parole is denied and high money bail set
in many cases in which the judge apparently desires to
impose preventive detention[30] which was neither authorized by the Code of Criminal Procedure,[31] nor based
on reliable indices of dangerousness,[32] nor even-
handed in its impact on defendants.[33] The bail process
is routinized.[34] This is indicated by manner in which
the criteria of bailability are applied without weighing the circumstances or situation of the defendant.[35]
The decision is based primarily on two factors,
seriousness of crime and prior record, rather than on
five or more factors which were specified under the
Code of Criminal Procedure.

A 1963 study entitled "The Manhattan Bail Project:
An Interim Report on the Use of Pretrial Parole,"[36]
indicates that defendants who have spent time in prison
awaiting trial are more likely to be convicted and more
likely to receive harsher sentences regardless of
whether they are first offenders or not. This is so
even if their social circumstances are acceptable in
terms of reliability for reappearance for trial.

The matter of isolating the criteria for
evaluating parole risk requires more
analysis than has so far been possible.
During the first year of operation, a
considerable degree of subjectivity in
this process was necessary and in fact
desirable. No doubt this will remain true
to a considerable extent, but analysis of
the common characteristics of successful
and unsuccessful parole cases may assist
in regularizing the process. Determinations as to what kind of people are good
or bad risks ought to rest on something
more solid than 'hunches.'[37]

The report continues:

The matter of availability of parole to
non-indigents also deserves consideration.
The parole experiment has been limited to
indigent defendants, but there would seem
to be no reason why others should be
excluded from a permanent system for the
sole reason that they can afford bail.
Such exclusion seems inherently wrong and
benefits only the professional bondsmen.[38]

What we observe here is the initial awareness of the
fact that the decision to allow bail as pretrial parole
solely on monetary terms is inherently discriminatory.
Chapter V will analyze how it violates the equal protection clause of the Constitution of the United States,
and is also a denial of due process.[39] What is significant is that the principal thrust of power, as the
Manhattan Bail Project did note, was money. In addition, the Project chose to provide assistance in non-
monetary forms of bail for the first time for those who
were indigent. What is significant in this Manhattan
Bail Project experiment, as is noted by Hans Zeisel in
an article in The Law and Society Review, is that on
the appointed day in court the proportion of defendants
released on non-monetary conditions who appeared for
trial was equal to those who had posted a monetary
bail.[40] This indicates that basing the decision to
release a defendant prior to trial on monetary considerations is inadequate. What is important in these
procedures for obtaining release is that defendants
released after posting some kind of surety, even when
it is not their own, were no more or less inclined to
show up for trial, with the result that homes,

property and goods, bankbooks of friends and relatives were at times forfeit.

According to the report entitled "Bail and Parole Jumping in Manhattan in 1967,"[41] comparing bail settings in felony cases in 1960 and 1967 reveals that the percentage of accused felons being released rose from 45% to 55%, primarily because of a sharp increase in the experimental use of release on recognizance (ROR). While there was a downward shift in the amount of bail required, there was also a marked decrease in the ability to post bail at any given level. What is significant in this series of 1967 statistics is that the overall rate of willful non-appearance was 13.9% in total. This breaks down to 10.5% for felony cases, 11.0% for misdemeanors, and 23.6% for violation.[42] It is noted that the rate of non-appearance increased with the diminished seriousness of the crime charged.

In substance, the report, "Bail and Parole Jumping. . . ," argues for the increase of release on recognizance which is a form of release to one's self on one's own say-so, having met criteria of acceptability to the court. However, it is important to note that this is really not a form of monetary bail. It is significant to note that in the classic original concept of bailability, defendants were released to someone in the community. This was seen in Chapter One. A careful examination of the Manhattan Bail Project of 1963 reveals that while they entitled their program a form of release on recognizance, in actuality the defendants released under this program were released to the Vera Institute of Justice.

Since, as we have noted, the Legal Aid Society's study of cases for the years 1970 and 1971, published in 1972, indicates that defendants spending time before trial in prison are still more likely to be convicted and more likely to receive harsher sentences,[43] then this analysis forces us to ask and examine what progress has been made in those intervening years between the Vera and Legal Aid Studies.

Bail or Jail?

Throughout the controversy over bail, the central issue has been the right to bail. There are two distinct questions involved. First, is bail an absolute right in all non-capital cases before conviction? Second, what constitutes excessive bail? The question of excessive bail is stated very briefly in the Eighth

Amendment of the Constitution of the United States, and is also a constitutional provision of the Constitution of the State of New York.[44] It has been suggested that the constitutional right to reasonable bail, that is, not excessive, implies the existence of a right to be admitted to bail in all non-capital crime cases. This point has not been tested before the Supreme Court since federal statutes and state statutes generally guarantee some such admission to bail.[45] There is some precedent that the right to bail is statutory and where it is statutory, state legislatures have the right to make offenses non-bailable as well as bailable.[46] The rights of the defendants in criminal proceedings are presently protected by Rule 46 of the Federal Rules of Criminal Procedure.[47] In many states the right to bail is secured by a state constitutional provision establishing that all non-capital cases shall be bailable before conviction. The United States Constitution and that of New York State which follows the United States Constitution, have no such proviso. Therefore, while the right to bail is protected, in New York State there is no clear stipulation that it is a right in all non-capital cases. Therefore, there is a discrepancy. The right to be bailed in all non-capital cases is clearly spelled out by some states[48] in their constitutions, and in other states it is statutory.[49] A recent decision of the United States Court of Appeals is relevant on this particular aspect of the bail problem.

> Neither the Eighth Amendment nor the Fourteenth Amendment, requires that everyone charged with a state offense must be given his liberty pending trial. While it is inherent in our American concept of liberty that a right to bail shall generally exist, this has never meant that a state must make every criminal offense subject to such a right, or that the right provided as to offenses made subject to bail must be so administered that every accused shall always be able to secure his liberty pending trial. Traditionally, and acceptedly, there are offenses of a nature as to which a state may refuse to make provision for a right to bail.[50]

Federally, bail is not an absolute right even though the right to bail which is not excessive is. The right to bail must be accorded by each state according to its own interpretation of whether it is a constitutional or statutory prerogative and what categories of offense permit bail.

Looking at the bail phenomenon in the legal context, the following observations are pertinent. Bail is provided by procedural law.[51] The law is enforced by persons of special statuses through means that may include the use of force with a low probability of retaliation, a condition that does not characterize customs and mores.[52]

There is a different legal setting for bail than for trial. While there are rules of procedure mutually arrived at[53] by the principal agents in the arraignment proceeding, namely the prosecuting attorney, defense counsel and the presiding judge, they are highly discretionary.[54] The rules lack the rigorous safeguards of the trial procedure. As Foote remarks, "The expectation of all connected with the administration of criminal justice -- police, jailer, prosecutor, defense, judge and probation office -- prejudge the case a failure."[55]

The defendant's achievement of bailed status is dependant on procedural law. When a person is arrested and accused of a crime, he enters the status of defendant or accused in the criminal justice system. The transition is from one status to another, innocent to innocent accused, or innocent to defendant.

If the right to bail adheres in this status of innocent accused or defendant, what are the factors involved in granting this right, since evidence shows that not all of this status receive bail? First, it is necessary to recognize that the status of defendant is essentially a passive one. The defendant is acted upon by those Blumberg calls agent mediators.[56] Those agent mediators, namely the judge, prosecutor and defense counsel, have the duty to invoke the bail machinery. Bail will be withheld or granted based upon an adversary procedure or contest in which the prosecutor and defense counsel will argue for or against release prior to trial.

Is it possible to have equitable application of the normative criteria of bail in criminal proceedings? The normative criteria are the formal categories of bail evaluation. In the State of New York these are: the nature of the offense, the projected penalty to be imposed, the probability of appearance or flight, the pecuniary and social condition of the defendant, and the apparent nature and strength of proof and probability of conviction. These categories are set out in the Code of Criminal Procedure.[57] Are these criteria applicable to a given status, namely defendant, in such a way as to be legally equitable and socially just, and not based solely on money?

It is important to note that in terms of statutory law rather than procedural law, the probability of appearance or flight is the only statutory norm for bail. Theoretically, if the defendant agrees to appear, he must be released.[58] If not, he must be detained in circumstances guaranteed to assure his attendance at trial. All other factors are evaluative of the likelihood of appearance as stated by the defendant i.e., procedural. It is in this area of judicial latitude that the majority of problems in the determination of bail arise. Theoretically, the decision of the judge is based upon procedural criteria as indicators of reliability that the defendant will appear. However, the judge utilizes these criteria or not as he sees fit. He is not required to explain his decision.

The following table shows some discretionary factors which judges include in their determination of the defendants' reliability.

The Situation of the Defendant

The criteria established by the Code of Criminal Procedure will govern the analysis of the 878 selected cases from the files of the Legal Aid Society in the City of New York. These cases, covering felony, misdemeanor and violation of the law in the period April, May and June, 1970, provide a sample of the bail procedures from a careful documentary analysis of each individual case for application of the criteria of bailability.

First, is there a correspondence between the nature of offense and the probability of the defendant's appearance? Legally there is a statutory correspondence between the gravity of the charge and the apparent reliability of appearance. The laws of most states allow bail only in non-capital cases. The belief is that in cases such as homicide the defendant

is more likely not to appear.[60] The nature of the
offense charged against the defendant is an abstract
category which may bear little or no resemblance to the
facts pertinent to arrest. For example, one may have
stolen a truck but be charged with the unauthorized
interstate transportation of merchandise. Such varia-
tions are arrangements worked out between the defense
counsel and the prosecutor as Sudnow points out.[61] The
charge is a negotiable commodity.[62] While formally the
charge is supposed to bear upon the defendant's reliability of appearance, in fact it often bears not a
whit of resemblance to the details of the case, and in
this sense is not relevant.[63]

Second, is there a correspondence between the
nature of the penalty and reliability of appearance?
Legally there is a correspondence between the category
of the crime and the penalty to be imposed. The
assumption is that the harsher the penalty, the more
likely one is to avoid the jurisdiction of the court.
There is no firm evidence to support this. Schaffer,
in his study, noted there was no clear correspondence
between failure to appear and the severity of possible
punishment.[64] Wolfgang has shown that convicted felons
did not contemplate the penalty for failure as they had
convinced themselves that their schemes would succeed.
Additionally, in crimes of passion consequences do not
figure in the action at all.[65]

The category of the crime charge and the nature of
the penalty are legally connected within a specific
range of severity, such as homicide in the first degree,
second degree or in the third degree. The penalty
ranges from death to a statutory "life" term. Con-
versely, there is no evidence to support the contention
that one is more likely to flee the jurisdiction of the
court because of a specific penalty. The fact that the
State of Massachusetts allows bail in selected capital
cases sustains this.[66]

Third, is there a correspondence between the
financial condition of the defendant and reliability
of the defendant's appearance? Under the then extant
Code of Criminal Procedure almost all pretrial releases
were secured by bail bond, as several studies of bail
bondsmen have revealed.[67] The assumption has been that
if you put up your savings or property you are not
likely to flee, as you would lose them. Naturally this
militated against the release of those who had no real
property or accumulated capital.

TABLE I59

Rank of Demographic Factors Utilized by Probation
Officers for Recommendations and District Court Judges
for Sentencing Alternatives, According to Probability
and Contingency Coefficient Values, 500 Federal
Offenders, Northern District of California, 9/64 to
8/65.

DEMOGRAPHIC FACTORS	PROBATION OFFICERS' RANKING	DISTRICT COURT JUDGES' RANKING
PRIOR RECORD	1	3
CONFINEMENT STATUS	2	2
NUMBER OF ARRESTS	3	4
OFFENSE	4	1
LONGEST EMPLOYMENT	5	5
OCCUPATION	6	8
NUMBER OF MONTHS EMPLOYED	7	6
INCOME	8	10
LONGEST RESIDENCE	9	7
MILITARY HISTORY	10	9
NUMBER OF RESIDENCE CHANGES	11	17
DISTANCE TO OFFENSE	12	14
NUMBER OF ALIASES	13	24
MARITAL STATUS	14	11
LEGAL REPRESENTATION	15	13
WEAPONS AND VIOLENCE	16	15
FAMILY CRIMINALITY	17	21
PLEA	18	18
EDUCATION	19	12
CHURCH ATTENDANCE	20	16
NARCOTICS USE	21	23
SEX	22	19
ALCOHOL INVOLVEMENT	23	25
CRIME PARTNERS	24	20
HOMOSEXUALITY	25	26
RACE	26	28
AGE	27	22
RELIGION	28	27

The formal categories for bailability place pecuniary and social conditions as one factor. It is important to note this combination of factors because it shows that the system for the administration of justice is able to differentiate legal criteria but combines others with which it is less familiar.

Is there a correspondence between the social condition of the defendant and reliability of appearance? The Code of Criminal Procedure does not spell out the meaning of the term "social condition." In practice this includes job, education, family, residence, previous record and potential dangerousness of the accused, previous record and potential dangerousness of the accused, to mention only the most common factors asked about in court or raised by the attorneys (see Table I). Legally, lack of fixed residence brings one under the vagrancy laws as a drifter or rootless person. No family ties, lack of education, while not crimes are indices of lack of social integration in the eyes of the court. These factors often exist in connection with vagrancy as the Philadelphia Skid Row Project has shown.[68] The American ethos has, since Captain John Smith's dictum at Jamestown, "If you don't work you don't eat," regarded lack of gainful employment as suspect. As Weber showed in The Protestant Ethic and the Spirit of Capitalism,[69] the inner worldly asceticism of the entrepreneur was a sign of divine predilection revealed in gainful employment and successful accumulation of wealth. The social gospel and the gospel of wealth in the 19th century placed great stock in job, education and community roots as barometers of a social status.

Fourth, is there a correspondence between the apparent nature and strength of proof regarding probable conviction and reliability of the defendant's appearance? Legally such an evaluation, a disposition of the case by subjective judgment without the benefit of trial and trial safeguards is prejudicial. It amounts to saying we cannot let you go because we have enough to prove you are guilty. This is distinctly different from the grand jury indictment which says there is enough data to warrant trial. As a formal canon of procedure this is open to question. Informally it is often used to pressure the defendant by indicating that the prosecution has the evidence it needs so time should not be wasted on delaying tactics which are hindering the efficiency of the court. It is this kind of procedure which is used in plea bargaining, according to Sudnow.[70] The question of proof favors the presumption of guilt, implying that if you are released you will flee, rather than if you are released you will seek to clear yourself. That bail-jump rate figures are as low as they are, regardless of the category of offense, indicates that there is no direct correlation between apparent proof of guilt and willingness to enter trial.[71]

It is essential to see the bail categories as evaluative, as conceptual equipment by which lawyers, judges and other criminal court functionaries organize their activities. It is a form of "perceptual short-hand" as Skolnick noted in Justice Without Trial.[72] Table II demonstrates the two ideal types in the bail risk profile. The favorable risk is one who has long and steady employment, strong family roots with wife and children at home, stable residence pattern, is able to produce references, is a defendant on a minor charge and has no previous record. While on the other hand, the unfavorable risk is one who has a long history of criminal activity on record, is charged with a serious crime, has an unfavorable residence pattern, can offer no, or unsatisfactory, references, has a history of family instability and lack of stable employment. It is in the marginal category between the ideal favorable and unfavorable bail risk that the greatest evaluative difficulties occur. This is true for the Criminal Procedure Law as well as the old Code.

TABLE II

IDEAL BAIL RISK PROFILE

Favorable Risk Ranking	(Marginal Risk)	Unfavorable Risk Ranking
1. Employment		1. Record
2. Family		2. Charge
3. Residence	?	3. Residence
4. References		4. References
5. Charge		5. Family
6. Record		6. Employment

What combinations of these factors make one a marginal risk? This is not to say that any risk profiles may act atypically. The solution has been that one is a favorable risk if he can afford monetary bail and an unfavorable one if he cannot. This practice of determining worth on a financial basis alone which is a denial of equal protection, has been struck down by the Supreme Court in <u>Griffin</u> vs. <u>Illinois</u> where an indigent was denied a transcript he could not afford to purchase.[73]

Chapter III will set forth how in the adversarial contest between defense counsel and prosecutor, the defense counsel makes use of the "good risk ranking" and the prosecutor uses the "poor risk ranking" in the bail setting process.

Summary

An examination of the literature on bail reveals that there is no major contemporary sociological study of the bail phenomenon in the United States. Most of the literature on bail in the United States, and some comparative work, has emerged since Dorothy L Tompkins' bibliography, <u>Bail in The United States</u>, first appeared in 1964.[75] This study needs to be brought up to date. The classic treatises by Sir Edward Coke[76] and Arthur L. Beeley[77] have yet to be rivaled. The majority of the studies on the social implications of bail has come forth from law schools and legal studies concerned with the relationship of bail and pretrial detention, bail and indigency, such as Caleb Foote's study[78] and the studies of Ares and Sturz;[79] Ares, Rankin and Sturz.[80] Nineteen-hundred and sixty-four and 1965 conferences on bail held in Washington, D.C.[81] indicated the growing concern with the social aspects of bail. From this series of conferences popular accounts by Goldfarb[82] and Ramsey Clark,[83] to mention just two, have emerged. The remainder of the literature has appeared in law journals such as the <u>Yale Law Review</u>,[84] <u>Pennsylvania Law Review</u>,[85] and the <u>Harvard Civil Rights and Civil Liberties Review</u>.[86]

Our concern here is not with the phenomenon of indigency nor with the cause and effect relationship between bail and pretrial detention as a form of punishment, but rather with what Erving Goffman calls the moral aspects of career. He defines this as the regular sequence of changes that career entails in the person's self and in his framework of imagery for judging himself and others.

The moral career of a person of a given
social category involves a standard
sequence of changes in his way of con-
ceiving of selves, including importantly
his own. . . .Each moral career, and
behind this each self occurs within the
confines of an institutional system whether
a social establishment such as a . . .
complex of personal or professional relationships. The self, then can be seen as
something that resides in the arrangements
prevailing in a social system for its
members. The self in this sense is not a
property of the person to whom it is
attributed, but dwells rather in the
pattern of social control that is exerted
in connection with the person by himself
and those around him. This special kind
of institutional arrangement does not so
much support the self as constitute it.[87]

The defendant's unique situation becomes abstract in the
complex interplay of criminal justice. How this occurs
will be seen in Chapter III.The defendant has acquired
a particular status as defendant and status rights --
the right to counsel, the right to be silent, the right
to a speedy trial. The extent and manner in which these
rights will be used depends upon how the defendant
evaluates his status or has it evaluated by counsel.
The choices in this evaluation are basically two: plead
guilty or plead not guilty. By pleading guilty[88] one
gives up the right to trial, to bail, to silence,
though usually not to counsel. By pleading guilty one
takes on the status of "convicted." By pleading not
guilty, one takes on the status of defendant in the
adversary procedure. Refusing to plead guilty, the
defendant states his innocence. Refusing to confess,
to "cop a plea," the defendant is demanding full
constitutional rights to which he is entitled by a
trial process to retain his innocence. This, however,
is interfering with the efficiency of the court's
administration which is based on high conviction rate
primarily from guilty pleas. This refusal to plead
guilty places the accused in a hostile relationship
with the criminal court system as represented by the
prosecutor. Abraham S. Blumberg remarks

The 'adversary system' and the 'presumption
of innocence' are comprised in the framework of the formal court process itself.

They are supplanted by a non-adversary,
accusatory system which actually favors
a presumption of guilt.[89]

Blumberg has also shown that those who refuse to plead
guilty and go to trial, if convicted receive harsher
penalties.[90] This accords with Foote's earlier remark
"that the expectation of all connected with the administration of criminal justice. . .prejudge the case a
failure."[91]

While it cannot be gainsaid that crime is legally
defined as a violation of the laws of the society, it
is also important to note that crime is socially determined. It is the result of the violation of laws
established by a segment of the society and applied to
the whole. By what society sanctions under law, it
also defines its criminal as its deviant from the
law.[92] The nature of the offense at law may be viewed
very differently in the eyes of the communities which
compose society. This is typically the case in
"victimless crimes," such as playing the numbers,
gambling, prostitution and consensual homosexuality.[93]
There are even conflicting standards of value. Since
the City of New York is not a homogeneous society, it
is hard to define crime as Durkheim did, as that which
offends the collective consciousness of the community.[94]

There is no examination legally why one might
commit a certain crime. The court then is the deter-
miner of whether one did or did not offend a particular
criminal statute, either by admission or trial and the
penalty for such offense. Criminal law and criminal
procedure are legal, rational formulations. They are
concerned with the facts of violation of a law and the
mandate given them to see that laws are upheld and
enforced, and where violations occur suitably punished.
This legal rational procedure is highly sophisticated,
but there is still a quality of "cadi" justice about
it, as Max Weber noted.

> The bourgeois strata have generally tended
> to be intensely interested in a rational
> procedural system, and therefore in a
> systematized and unambiguous formal and
> purposefully constructed substantive law
> which eliminates both obsolete traditions
> and arbitrariness, and in which rights can
> have their source exclusively in general
> norms. Such a systematically codified law

was thus demanded by the English Puritans,
the Roman plebians, and the German
bourgeoisie of the 15th century. But in
all these cases such a system was still a
long way off.[95]

It is important for us to recognize that we still lack
such a rational procedural system which is able to
eliminate obsolete traditions and arbitrariness. And
in the light of our increasing social sophistication
it is questionable whether, as Weber pointed out, we
can have rights stated exclusively as norms. The
Eighth Amendment to the Constitution of the United
States articulates a right exclusively in terms of a
general norm, "that bail shall not be excessive."[96]
At present we are beginning to see the importance of
understanding the meaning of this right, not in terms
of a general norm but rather in an analysis of its
specific application.

FOOTNOTES

1. John Jennings, The Flow of Arrested Defendants Through New York City Criminal Court in 1968. New York: The Rand Institute, 1970, p. 27.

2. Frank W. Miller, Prosecution: The Decision to Charge a Suspect with a Crime. Boston: Little Brown & Co., 1969, pp. 24-42.

3. The Code of Criminal Procedure. The State of New York, Rev. Ed., 1962, Sections 550-556. See also Criminal Procedure Law of New York. Irving Shapiro, ed. New York: Gould Publications, 1971. Part III, Title ·P·, articles 500-540.30.

4. Ruth S. Cavan, Criminology. New York: Thomas Y. Crowell, 3rd ed., 1962, pp. 319-322.

5. "Gamelyn" in Middle English Verse Romances, Donald B. Sands (ed.). New York: Holt, Reinhart & Winston, Inc., 1966, pp. 154-181.

6. "Freedom At A Price. Bail Bondsmen Wield Surprising Power, Stir Growing Controversy." The Wall Street Journal, Thursday, October 7, 1971, p. 1.

7. Ares, Rankin and Sturz, "The Manhattan Bail Project - An Interim Report in the Use of Pre-Trial Parole." 38 New York University Law Review, 1963, pp. 67-92.

8. The Code of Criminal Procdure, Section 552. Vol. 66 in McKinney's Consolidated Laws of New York. Brooklyn, N.Y.: Edward Thompson, 1968 ed.

9. Andrew Schaffer, The Problem of Overcrowding in the Detention Institutions of New York City: An Analysis of Causes and Recommendations to Alleviation (Mimeo). New York: The Vera Institute of Justice, January 1969, pp. 8-9.

10. John Bellamy et al vs. The Judges and Justices Authorized to Sit in the New York City Criminal Court Plaintiffs Memorandum. New York: The Legal Aid Society, March 1972.

11. Fred P. Graham, The Self-Inflicted Wound. New York: The Macmillan Co., 1970, pp. 18-20.

12. Gideon vs. Wainwright 372 U.S. 335 83 S. Ct. 792 (1963).

13. Griffin vs. Illinois 351 U.S. 12, 76 S. Ct. 585 (1956).

14. Escobedo vs. Illinois 378 U.S. 478 S. Ct. 1758 (1964). See also Miranda vs. Arizona 384, U.S. 436, 86 S. Ct. 1602 (1966).

15. See Footnote 10.

16. "State Senate Committee Charges City Lags on Proposals for Reforms at Tombs." The New York Times, Thursday, February 4, 1971. See also, "Prison Criticized by Vanden Heuvel," The New York Times, February 4, 1971. "Waiting for Their Days in Court Can - and Does - Take Many Months in Jail," The New York Times, Sunday, December 6, 1970. "Justice is Slow and Unsure in Nation's Busy Courts," The New York Times, Monday, March 8, 1971.

17. "Awaiting Their Day in Court," The New York Times, Sunday, December 6, 1970.

18. "Judiciary and Jails Blamed by Panel for Tombs Suicide." The New York Times, November 18, 1970.

19. "Awaiting Their Day in Court," The New York Times, Sunday, December 6, 1970.

20. U.S. Congress, Federal Bail Reform Act, 18 Congress #3146, 1966.

21. Criminal Procedure Law of New York, Irving Shapiro, ed. New York: Gould Publications, 1971. loc cit.

22. The Criminal Procedure Law of the State of New York effective September 1971, authorizes eight categories of bail or bond not all of which require money. These are cash bail, an insurance company bail bond, a secured surety bond, a secured appearance bond, a partially secured appearance bond, an unsecured surety bond, and an unsecured appearance bond. Cash bail means a sum of money, in the amount designated in an order fixing bail, posted by a principal or by another person on his behalf with a court or other authorized public servant, or agency, upon the condition that such money will become forfeit

to the people of the State of New York if the
innocent accused does not comply with the direc-
tions of a court requiring his attendance at the
criminal action.

Bail bond means a written undertaking, executed
by one or more obligors, that the accused
designated in such instrument will, while at
liberty as a result of an order fixing bail and
of the posting of the bail bond in satisfaction
thereof, appear in a designated criminal action
when required or be amenable to the orders and
processes of the court, and that in the event of
failure to do so the obligors will pay to the
people of the State of New York a specified sum
of money as prescribed in the order fixing bail.

An appearance bond means a bail bond in which only
the obligor is the principal. A surety bond is
one in which the obligor or obligors consist of
one or more sureties or of one or more surieties
and the principal. An insurance company bail bond
means a surety bond, executed in the form prescribed by the superintendent of insurance, in
which the surety-obligor is a corporation licensed
by the superintendent of insurance to engage in the
business of executing bail bonds.

A secured bail bond means a bail bond secure
either by personal property which is not exempt
from execution and which over and above all
liabilities and encumbrances, has a value equal
to or greater than the total amount of the undertaking; or real property having a value at least
twice the total amount of the undertaking.

A partially secured bail bond means one secured
only by a deposit of a sum of money not exceeding
ten percent of the total amount of the undertaking.
An unsecured bail bond means one other than an
insurance company bond, not secured by any deposit
of or lien upon property.

   Section 510.30 of the <u>Criminal Procedure
   Law</u> states

      'To the extent that the issuance of an
      order of recognizance or bail and the
      terms thereof are matters of <u>discretion</u>
      /underlining mine/ rather than of law,

69

an application must be determined on the basis of the following factors and criteria:

(a) . . .the kind and degree of control or restriction that is necessary to secure his court attendance when required. In determining that matter, the court must, on the basis of available information consider and take into account. . .

eight factors. These are: first, the accused's character, reputation, habits and mental condition; second, his employment and financial resources; third, his family ties and the length of his residence if any in the community; fourth, his criminal record if any; fifth, his previous record if any in responding to court appearances when required or with respect to flight to avoid prosecution; sixth, if he is a defendant, the weight of evidence against him in the pending criminal action and any other factor indicating probability or improbability of conviction; seventh, if he is a defendant, the sentence which may be imposed; eighth, the likelihood that the defendant would be a danger to society or to himself if at liberty during the pendancy of action.

Of course one cannot be sure of a judge's reasons for rejecting a recommendation for pretrial parole because they are rarely stated explicitly.

23. Anne Rankin, "The Effect of Pretrial Detention." New York University Law Review 39 June 1964, No. 4, p. 641.

24. C. Ares and H. Sturz, "Bail and the Indigent Accused," Crime and Delinquency 8 January, 1962, pp. 12-20.

25. Patricia Wald, "Pretrial Detention and Ultimate Freedom," New York University Law Review 39 June, 1964, No. 4.

26. Erving Goffman, Stigma. Englewood Cliffs, N.J.: Prentice Hall, Inc., 1963, pp. 41-44.

27. *Code of Criminal Procedure*, Section 550, case note 2.

28. Ibid., case note 4. See also note 22.

29. Ibid., Sections 550-553.

30. *Bail and Summons: 1965*. New York: Vera Institute of Justice, August 1966, p. 93. The decision of the Court of Appeals of the State of New York on use of bail for preventive detention.

31. *The Code of Criminal Procedure*, Sections 550-556.

32. *The Criminal Procedure Law*, Section 510.30 2(a) (c). Under the Criminal Procedure Law the determination of dangerousness is to be made on the basis of the defendant's character, reputation, habits, mental condition, previous criminal record (convictions and charges) and the current charges. No study has ever been made of the relative importance of these factors in predicting dangerousness. Even with all this information available, the judge has no evaluative criteria. See note 66. See also Schaffer, *The Problem of Overcrowding. . .*, p. 3 f.

33. "Judge Supported on Prostitution," *The New York Times*, August 1, 1971.

34. A. Schaffer, *Bail and Parole Jumping in Manhattan in 1967*. New York: Vera Institute of Justice, August 1970, pp. 47-48.

35. Ares, Rankin and Sturz, "The Manhattan Bail Project. . . ." p. 70.

36. Ares, Rankin and Sturz, "The Manhattan Bail Project. . . ." pp. 70-71.

37. Ibid., p. 91.

38. Loc cit., p. 91.

39. Lockhart, Kamisar and Choper, *Constitutional Rights and Liberties*. St. Paul: The West Publishing Co., 3rd ed. Appendix B, pp. 22-23.

40. Hans Zeisel, "Methodological Problems and Techniques in Sociological Research," *Law and Society Review*, Vol. 2, No. 3, May 1968, pp. 504-508.

41. Schaffer, Bail and Parole Jumping. . ., pp. 304.

42. "Police Set Drive on Bail Jumpers," The New York Times, January 6, 1971.

43. Bellamy vs. Judges, hereinafter cited as "Legal Aid Study." See Tables 5, 7, 8, 15, 16, 20, 21 and 22.

44. The Constitution of the State of New York, Article 1, Section 5.

45. "Bail: An Ancient Practice Reexamined." 70 Yale Law Journal, pp. 966-977 (1961). Includes an appendix: State Laws Governing the Right to Bail.

46. See Foote, "The Administration of Bail in New York," pp. 696-698, esp. notes 9 through 20.

47. Federal Rules of Criminal Procedure. 3146, Section 46, Revised 1966.

48. Commonwealth of Massachusetts vs. Baker. Massachusetts makes homicide bailable under certain conditions. cf. fn. 66.

49. Caleb Foote, "A Study of the Administration of Bail in New York City." University of Pennsylvania Law Review, Vol. 106, 1958, p. 696, note 11.

50. Mastrian vs. Headman in Bail and Summons: 1965, p. 165.

51. Code of Criminal Procedure, Sections 550-556.

52. Jack P. Gibbs, "The Sociology of Law and Normative Phenomena," American Sociological Review, Vol. 31, No. 3, June 1966.

53. F. Suffet, "Bail Setting: A Study of Courtroom Interaction." Crime and Delinquency. October 1966, p. 322.

54. Abraham S. Blumberg, Criminal Justice, Chicago: Quadrangle Books, 1969, pp. 103-105.

55. Foote (ed.), "Studies in Bail," University of Pennsylvania Law Review, 1966, p. 288.

56. Blumberg, op. cit., p. 95.

57. Code of Criminal Procedure, Sections 550-556.

58. Bail and Summons: 1965, pp. 43-45.

59. Richard Quinney (ed.), Crime and Justice in Society. Boston: Little Brown & Co., 1969, p. 407.

60. "Supreme Court, 5-4, Bars Death Penalty As It Is Imposed Under Present Statutes." The New York Times, June 30, 1972, p. 1, headline.

61. D. Sudnow, "Normal Crimes: Sociological Features of the Penal Code in a Public Defender Office." Social Problems, 12 Winter, 1965, p. 265.

62. Blumberg, op. cit., p. 113-f.

63. Sudnow, op. cit., pp. 267-269.

64. Schaffer, Bail and Parole Jumping. . ., pp. 25-27,

65. M. Wolfgang, Patterns in Criminal Homicide. Philadelphia: University of Pennsylvania, 1958,

66. Commonwealth vs. Baker 343 Massachusetts 162. See also Chapter 276, Sections 42 to 57, Massachusetts Statutes.

67. Michael Pearl, "Hard Times in Bail Bond Row," New York, September 29, 1969, pp. 40-44. See Table, p. 43. Also, "The Bail Bond Scandal," The Saturday Evening Post, June 20, 1964; "Bail: Justice Far From All," New York Times Magazine, August 19, 1962, pp. 13-44.

68. C. Foote, "Vagrancy Type Law and Its Administration." 104, University of Pennsylvania Law Review, 1956, p. 615.

69. Max Weber, The Protestant Ethic and the Spirit of Capitalism. New York: The Free Press, 1963.

70. Sudnow, "Normal Crimes," p. 265.

71. Bail and Parole Jumping. . ., pp. 44-46.

72. Jerome Skolnick, Justice Without Trial. New York: John Wiley & Sons, Inc., pp. 42-44 and 46.

73. <u>Griffin</u> vs. <u>Illinois</u> 351, U.S. 12, 76 S. Ct. 585.

74. <u>U.S.</u> vs. <u>Bandy</u> 81 Supreme Court 197-8. 1960.
    See also <u>Ransom</u>, p. 18.

75. Dorothy L. Tompkins, <u>Bail in the United States</u>.
    Berkeley: Institute of Governmental Studies,
    University of California, ed. 1967.

76. Sir Edward Coke, <u>A Little Treatise of Baile and</u>
    <u>Maineprize</u>. London: William Cooke, 1637, Chapter
    One.

77. Arthur L. Beeley, <u>The Bail System in Chicago</u>
    (1927). Chicago: University of Chicago Press,
    1965.

78. C. Foote, "Vagrancy Type Law and Its Administra-
    tion." 104, <u>University of Pennsylvania Law</u>
    <u>Review</u> 1956, pp. 603-650.

79. C. Ares and H. Sturz, "Bail and the Indigent
    Accused," <u>Crime and Delinquency</u> 8 January, 1962,
    pp. 12-20.

80. Ares, Rankin and Sturz, "The Manhattan Bail
    Project - An Interim Report in the Use of Pre-
    trial Parole." 38 <u>New York University Law</u>
    <u>Review</u>, 1963, pp. 67-69ff.

81. <u>National Conference on Bail and Criminal Justice.</u>
    Washington, D.C.: April 1965, and <u>Bail and</u>
    <u>Summons: 1965</u>, New York: Vera Institute of Justice,
    August 1966, p. xxii.

82. Ronald Goldfarb, <u>Ransom: A Critique of the American</u>
    <u>Bail System</u>. New York: Harper and Row, 1965,
    p. 18f.

83. Ramsey Clark, <u>Crime in America</u>. New York: Simon
    and Shuster, 1970. See Chapter 18.

84. "Bail: An Ancient Practice Reexamined." 70 <u>Yale</u>
    <u>Law Journal</u>, pp. 966-977 (1961). Includes an
    appendix: State Laws Governing the Right to Bail.

85. Caleb Foote, "The Coming Crisis in Bail,"
    <u>University of Pennsylvania Law Review</u>, I, Vol.
    113, No. 7, May 1, 1965, pp. 959-999. II, Vol.
    113, No. 8, pp. 1125-1185.

86. Sam Ervin, Jr., "Preventive Detention: An Empirical Analysis," The Harvard Civil Rights, Civil Liberties Law Review, Vol. 3, March 1972, p. 292ff.

87. Erving Goffman, Asylums: Essays on the Social Situation of Mental Patients and Other Inmates. Garden City, N.Y.: Anchor Books, pp. 127-169.

88. D. Sudnow, "Normal Crimes: Sociological Features of the Penal Code in a Public Defender Office." Social Problems 12 Winter, 1965, pp. 255-276.

89. Blumberg, Criminal Justice, p. 6.

90. Ibid., pp. 31-32, Tables 2, 3.

91. See note 55.

92. Nicholas Kittrie, The Right to Be Different. Baltimore: Johns Hopkins Press, 1971, p. 21.

93. Norval Morris & G. Hawkins, The Honest Politician's Guide to Crime Control. Chicago: University of Chicago Press, 1970, p. 37.

94. Emile Durkheim, The Division of Labor in Society (1893) (trans. G. Simpson). New York: The Free Press, 1947, p. 152, note 3.

95. M. Weber, The Theory of Social and Economic Organization, Parsons ed. New York: Oxford University Press, 1947, p. 152, note 3.

96. See also "Magna Carta," in Milton Viorst, The Great Documents of Western Civilization. New York: Chilton Books, 1965, pp. 113-47; "The Habeas Corpus Act of 1679"; "The Bill of Rights of 1689."

CHAPTER III
THE AGENTS IN THE COURTROOM CONTEST

Introduction

Max Weber regarded Anglo-American law as distinctly
inferior in rationality to the systems derived from
Roman law.[1] Weber reasoned that common law is too akin
to the laymen's ideal of the practical, the expedient,
the expectable and rests too heavily on judicial
charisma. Roman law based continental systems are more
truly rational in their application of formulated rules
to the facts of particular controversies, he believed.[2]
Weber's analysis of law challenges one to ask the key
question: In the relationship of laws and society -
should decisions be uniformly and relentlessly according to formulà or is there room for the practical and
the expedient?

The Criminal Law of the State of New York contains
in its formulations on bail elements of the uniformly
rational and the expeditious. This chapter will examine bail in light of these two aspects as they are
presented by the principal courtroom agents.

First we shall examine the nature of rationality
and discretion in decision-making as presented by
Benjamin Cardozo. Second, we shall describe the
decision-making process at bail setting in its formal
and informal aspects. Third, we shall analyze the form
of the process.

Rationality and Discretion in Decision-Making

Benjamin Cardozo offered a framework for analysis
of judicial reasoning in his work, The Nature of the
Judicial Process.[3] He delineates four elements in the
judicial reasoning process: logic, precedent, history
and social utility.

First, logic encompassed generality, consistency,
deduction and induction. Generality in the legal frame
of reference refers to universals or propositions which
articulate norms. In the law norms are restatements of
the problem[4] as in the Eighth Amendment to the United
States Constitution "that bail shall not be excessive."
This is a general rule, it does not offer any application.

In legal logic consistency is essential to justice.
The difficulty arises in the application of differing
legal standards. Rule 46 of the Federal Rules of
Criminal Procedure states that a person arrested for

an offense not punishable by death shall be admitted to
bail. In most states this right is secured by a constitutional provision. The Constitution of the State
of New York has no such provision. The constitutions
of nine states do not have this provision: Georgia,
Maine, Maryland, Massachusetts, New Hampshire, New York,
North Carolina, Virginia and West Virginia.[5]

Logical deduction poses problems because the first
premises from which deduction begins may vary. In bail
proceedings the judge may choose to start from the
nature of the offense as his statutory first principle
or he may choose to start from the circumstances of the
defendant as his first principle.[6]

Logical induction in the legal process develops
from precedent and from the facts of the case. The
problems of precedent cause the problem of sameness.
Should bail for first degree assault with a weapon
always be set at the same amount? To what extent
should precedent be reexamined? Here the law employs
both principle and postulate in resolving each case.
It takes on the character of a scientific experiment
where the hypothesis, each time it is tested, has a
different set of variables. Generally the judge, as
experimenter, will not engage in extensive retrospective
questioning until he discovers that the rules for investigation no longer are applicable. At that point in
time the hypothesis and its variables will be re-
formulated.

Cardozo's second element is precedent.[7] A judge
in the arraignment part of criminal court has much less
time for decision-making than a trial judge or appellate judge, in relation to the number of cases he must
hear. Importantly, the decision at arraignment is:
shall the defendant be charged? If so, with what? At
trial it is a question of evidence and guilt, at
appeal the argument moves from evidence to procedure
and precedent. Precedents are embodied in formulas
which are then applied in future decision-making.[8]
Precedents are established and became conventions. To
move from conventions to the unconventional where day-
to-day life and judgment do not always conform to
precedent is to move to an inductive base where the
rules are less clear. The facts of daily life are part
of a social system which makes them intelligible. The
social system must be understood. Where social
phenomena serve as the facts of law, as Freund notes,[9]
special sensitivity and sophistication are called for

from our judges. The demands made in criminal court by victim and victimizer are shaped by the legal system itself. Here law, like sociology, builds on evidence.

Cardozo's third point is history. The judge can improve his interpretative ability through knowledge of legal narrative. This point shall be examined later.

Social utility is Cardozo's fourth element and an inclusive criterion.

> . . .In the law its limitations are near the surface. Law is a system for imposing a modicum of order on the disorder of human experience without disrespecting or suppressing a measure of spontaneity, diversity and disarray.[10]

The degree of order cannot always be argued from the principle of utility.[11] Some practices allow the judge to remove himself from the problems of value judgment which social utility would require. These practices include the following.

First, the judge must operate according to generally formulated rules. These can be legislative, judicial or experiential. In bail setting the general rule has been the amount of bail is determined by the category of the crime charged. This rule is not legislative nor judicial. It has evolved as the experience of judges and prosecutors. It is this general rule area which shall be examined in the ensuing chapters.

A second factor releasing the judge from value judgment is the nature of the procedure. At arraignment he is not trying the case. The judge is solely ". . .exercising control over his person /the defendant/ with respect to such accusatory instrument and of setting the course of further proceedings in the action."[12]

A third factor which circumscribes the judge is the form of sanction. The defendant may plead guilty or not guilty and the judge must decide how to proceed. Here the judge has flexibility. He has a wide area of discretion in his choice of response to pleas. To a plea of guilty to a felony he may only turn the case over to a superior court. To a plea of guilty to a misdemeanor or violation he may sentence up to a year in jail, a year on probation, a year on conditional release or a suspended sentence. To a plea of not guilty he may opt for two basic forms of control over the defendant. These include: detention or bail. Bail may take the form of release on recognizance,[13] cash bail[14] or a bail bond.[15]

In his choice of response to plea the judge is publicly assessed for either his creativity or his bias.[16] To be creative in a discipline is to remain within its general limits.[17] The judicial process puts a premium on order in the midst of change. There are innovative options for the judge at arraignment as noted. He is not so free to acquit as is a trial or appellate judge because he is circumscribed by the nature of his proceeding.

Judges in the arraignment court have been accused of bias in favor of detention.[18] The question here is among the alternatives available to the judge to "exercise control" over the defendant for what reasons are some alternatives chosen in preference to others? Much has been written describing the decisional statements of judges on sentencing.[19] The bail options decided and how they conform to the rationality of decision-making shall be described. Creativity and bias, insofar as they exist, are meaningful only in context. It must be kept in mind that the rationality discussed is subject to discretion as embodied in law, an important part in decision-making.[20]

A rational decision, for Wilkins, is defined as one which having regard to the information available maximizes the likelihood of obtaining the purpose desired,[21] in this case control of the defendant. There can be no rational decision without information. There can only be discretion in rational decision when all the information needed for that decision has been assessed. Is the bail setting process based on all information required by law? If so, it is rational and capable of discretion; if it is not, then it lacks rationality and retains elements of "cadi" justice.

In order to understand the legal rational decision-making process it must be described.

The Courtroom Scene

New York City Criminal Court, known as Manhattan Criminal Court, is located at 100 Centre Street in lower Manhattan. It occupies an entire city block and is connected with the Manhattan House of Detention, known as the "Tombs," where detained defendants traditionally await arraignment or trial and the sentenced await transfer to jail or prison.

As one enters the court building on Centre Street, inscriptions over the doors assure one of the presence of justice.

Equal and exact justice to all men of whatever state or persuasion.

Good faith is the foundation of justice.

The only true principle of humanity is justice.

Impartiality is the life of justice as justice is of good government.

Every place is safe to him who lives in justice.

Only the just man enjoys peace of mind.

Where law ends there tyranny begins.

A casual observation of those going in and out indicates that few people pause to read these inscriptions.

Entering the rotunda one observes numerous small enclaves of people. Policemen with defendants, defendants with lawyers, lawyers with bondsmen. People read the posted calendars - dittographed lists of arraignments, hearings, trials and appeals. These lists tell which judge is in what trial part or arraignment part and how many cases are on the list. There is a sense of waiting in the rotunda - to be called to arraignment, to witness, to testify, to plead.

Several corridors lead from the rotunda. At the end of one corridor is a room designated as "AR 1." "AR 1" is Arraignment, part one, where all adult felonies, misdemeanors and violations are first heard. Through the leather padded double doors of Room AR 1 with their single small glass window in each, is arraignment court.

The walls are paneled in oak, seven feet from floor to windowsill and topped by twelve-foot leaded windows. The high, beamed ceiling is a canopy for the

proceedings. As you sit in one of the oak spectator's
benches the courtroom scene unfolds. The judge sits
high over the proceedings enclosed in a paneled enclave
called "the bench." It is six feet high from floor to
ledge. He is surrounded by the symbols of his office.
The flag of the United States to his right and the flag
of the City to his left. Alongside him in stalls
slightly less elevated sit the court clerk to his right
and the stenographer to his left.

A few feet from the bench on the judge's right
hand is a table for defense counsel and benches. In
front of the judge is a table where the prosecutor
stands to make his prosecution and to which defendant
and his counsel are summoned by the "bridgeman," a
clerk in charge of calling the docket numbers and names
scheduled to appear before the judge.

On the judge's left hand is a row of benches where
defendants sit with policemen, with lawyers, and with
defendants. This bench is in the shape of the letter
"L." Starting at the top of the "L" along the wall to
the judge's left, it turns at a right angle toward the
center of the courtroom where a railing separates
participants from spectators. This inner section
occupies a little less than half the room.

The room is filled with activity. A door beyond
the defendants' "L"-shaped bench leads to detention
cells and interview rooms. A steady stream of defendants, policemen, lawyers, prosecutors, court attendants
and other officers of the court pass in and out while
proceedings go on.

The bridgeman calls a number and a name. The
prosecutor stands at the center table with his assembled
papers. The defendant approaches the bench with his
counsel. Defense counsel and prosecutor stand side by
side before the judge. The defendant to the left of
his counsel. To the prosecutor's right stands the
complainant if present in court; a policeman, a store
official or a victim.

The prosecutor begins with a statement of the
charge by section and paragraph of the Criminal Code,
called the "prosecutor's information,"[22] a "misdemeanor
complaint" or a "felony complaint."[23] If a prosecution
witness is present he is sworn in to testify to the
truth of the complaint. The defendant is called upon
to swear also. Defense counsel is then asked by the

bridgeman if he will waive the full reading of the
complaint. Defense counsel agrees and the defendant
is then asked by the judge to plead. If counsel enters
a plea of guilty to a felony, the defendant must be
remanded to Supreme Court which has felony jurisdiction.
If counsel enters a plea of guilty to a misdemeanor or
violation, then the defendant is sentenced by the judge
to a term of punishment which may be served in jail,
or probation or by conditional release.

If the defense counsel enters a plea of not guilty
to the charge, the bail process is begun because the
purpose of arraignment for the court is to "acquire and
exercise control over his /defendant's/ person with
respect to such accusatory instrument and of setting
the course of further proceedings in the action."24

The prosecutor responds to the defendant's plea
of not guilty by stating, "The people ask bail of 'x'
dollars." Defense counsel will either accept the bail
request of the prosecutor or ask for a reduction in
amount or form. If the prosecutor asks bail of $500,
defense counsel may request the court to accept $50 cash
bail which could be posted at once. Defense counsel
might ask that the defendant be released on his own
recognizance. A decision will be made by the judge.

The bridgeman then advises the defendant that he
is entitled to a trial before one judge, three judges
or a jury trial, and a free letter or a phone call.
This proceeding takes approximately four minutes if all
goes as prescribed. The process begins again with each
new defendant.

Each day between 10 A.M. and 4:30 or 5 P.M.,
between 100 and 150 adult defendants are arraigned.25

To understand how this formal arraignment proceeding moves so smoothly, we must examine the informal
pre-arraignment proceedings and what bearing they have
on the judge's decision.

The judicial decision to accept a plea of not
guilty, to release or detain results from the presentation by the prosecuting attorney and defense counsel
in an adversarial procedure. The Code of Criminal
Procedure specified five areas of examination for a
defendant's bailability. These are: 1) the nature of
the offense; 2) nature of the penalty; 3) probability
of appearance or flight; 4) social and pecuniary

condition of the defendant; 5) apparent nature and strength of proof and probability of conviction.[26]

These five criteria are to be the framework for the judge's rational decision, at arraignment, to release pending trial or detain in lieu of bail. When the content information of these criteria is lacking, can the judge maximize the likelihood of obtaining the desired purpose? Evidence contained in the following chapters would indicate maximization is unlikely.

These five criteria are examined before the judge in the formal arraignment proceeding. While the formal arraignment proceeding resembles a trial, it lacks the procedural safeguards of a trial. There is no jury. There is no right to challenge evidence, to cross-examine, to call witnesses or to request a mistrial. Until 1973, there were no established legal safeguards for the defendant in the pre-arraignment negotiations of prosecutor and defense counsel, where these same criteria are thrashed out in the determination of plea and terms of bail.

The Prosecutor's Formal Role

The prosecutor, a staff member of the District Attorney's Office, begins the formal arraignment encounter by stipulating the nature of the offense against the Penal Code by its section and subsection numbers. He may then describe the circumstances surrounding the nature of the offense. These may include violence, resisting arrest, use of weapon or drugs.

The prosecutor may then describe the prior record of the defendant which will include number and frequency of arrests, their nature and disposition. This information he will have acquired from the Report of the Office of Probation through the State's information and intelligence file. The data appear on "Yellow Sheet" because it is on yellow paper.

The prosecutor in his presentation will have covered at least three of the five criteria of bailability -- the nature of the offense, the apparent nature and strength of proof and probability of conviction, plus something of the social condition of the defendant from the "Yellow Sheet" if one exists.

STATE OF NEW YORK
CODE OF CRIMINAL PROCEDURE
ARRAIGNMENT

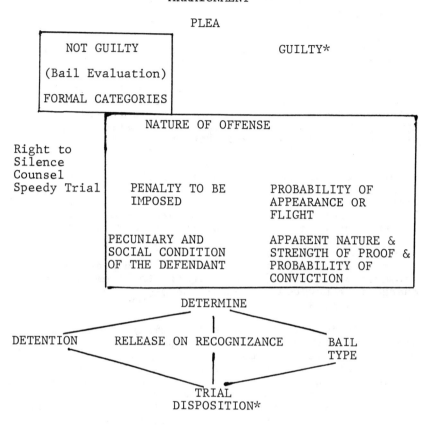

TABLE I

The Prosecutor's Informal Role

At that point in the arraignment when the defendant must choose how to plead, the criteria juncture in the criminal justice process is reached. Will the defendant affirm his innocence or guilt? The prosecutor presents his case in such a way that he will, where possible, obtain a plea of guilty.[27]

The substance of this critical courtroom plea is determined in the pre-arraignment meeting between defense counsel and prosecutor. Let us consider this hypothetical case. A defendant is arrested for possession of more than one-eighth ounce of heroin. Three counts may be lodged against this defendant. First, he may be charged with felonious possession of a narcotic drug. Second, he may be charged with felonious possession with intent to sell. Both counts carry prison terms over one year upon conviction. Third, unlawful possession of a narcotic drug is a misdemeanor with penalty less than a year.[28] As a result of preliminary discussion between defense and prosecution, the defendant may be offered the opportunity to plead to the third count. This depends on the strength of evidence. If it is agreed, then the third charge is announced in court, the defense pleads guilty and the judge sentences.

It is important to note that misdemeanors and violations are in the jurisdiction of the Criminal Court. Felonies must be heard in Supreme Court. A misdemeanor plea enables the case to be completed for the Criminal Court promptly as court of jurisdiction. A felony plea means a continuance to Supreme Court. While this is acceptable it is costly to the court and no defendant will plead to a more serious charge with greater penalty unless circumstances are most unusual. If he chooses to plead not guilty then bail must be set.

As Blumberg notes,[29] the multiplicity of counts with which a defendant may be charged allows for negotiation. Since the charges possess penalties ranging in severity from several years to several months, the prosecutor holds a powerful position in his freedom to choose the charge which shall be presented. There is therefore a logical connection between the nature of offense charged and the penalty to be imposed which is the second category for consideration.

86

The nature of the penalty has been considered pertinent to a bail decision because it has been assumed that the more severe the penalty on conviction, the more likely the defendant is not to appear for trial. Schaffer's study reveals there is no direct correspondence between the nature of the penalty and the likelihood of appearance.[30] Where a plea of guilty cannot be obtained, then the prosecutor will argue from the same criteria against bail as he sees these criteria indicating the probability of flight. When a plea of not guilty is entered the prosecutor will bear in mind that the defendant refused to plead guilty, to cooperate with the speedy administration of justice. This reluctance is considered a hostile act and will have some bearing on what the prosecution asks for bail in the case, and what kind, if any, should be allowed. The final determination is made by the judge. The judge, however, relies heavily on the prosecutor, as Suffet notes, and will accept his determination over that of defense counsel.[31]

In his argument against pretrial release, the prosecutor will try to emphasize the negative characteristics in the social and pecuniary condition of the defendant as far as they exist. These social and financial conditions are the starting point for the defense counsel's presentations at arraignment.

Defense Counsel's Formal Role

Defense counsel will develop the positive aspects of the defendant's biography - job, education, family life, military service - as much as he can while stressing whatever circumstances may mitigate the charge against his client. He does not declare his client's innocence but operates on the presumption of it and the responsibility of the prosecution to disprove it.

What is being argued before the bench in the few moments available is how to proceed. Defense counsel will advise against a guilty plea unless the prosecution indicates such a strong case that a trial would result in a harsher disposition as Blumberg notes,[32] or if a guilty plea to a lesser charge is most advantageous to his client.

Where defense counsel advises against a guilty plea, he will argue that the defendant should be released pending trial because of his satisfactory

social profile. One of the most important aspects of
the fourth evaluative category for bailability - social
and pecuniary circumstances of the defendant - is that
it places together these two undefined areas, social
and economic, under the heading of "circumstances."

The social circumstances of the defendant have
been seen traditionally by the prosecution as the
contents of the Report of the Office of Probation and
the "Yellow Sheet."[33] Prosecution has not concerned
itself with the economic life of the defendant. This
has been left to the defendant, his counsel and the
bondsman, if needed, as will be seen.

Defense Counsel's Informal Role

Defense counsel seeks to learn as much about the
defendant as possible in a pre-arraignment interview
with his client. It will help him decide if the
defendant is a favorable risk for bail. It will help
him negotiate a better plea.

Defense counsel does not have at his disposal for
indepth biographical research the kind of staff and
record-keeping system which serve the prosecutor in the
criminal justice system. Defense counsel is entitled
to a copy of the "Yellow Sheet" which the prosecutor
also receives. He receives a copy of the charges or
complaint as well. The gathering of data on his client
is carried out by the defense counsel in the time between his receiving the case and arraignment. In this
time he must interview the defendant, attempt to verify
as much data as he can by telephone and meeting with
the prosecutor at a pre-arraignment negotiating
session. Some factors weigh more heavily than others
in obtaining release once a plea of not guilty is
decided.

A key factor in bailability is: "Are you employed?" A defendant who holds a job manifests some
attachments in the community which would make him a
good risk. His job would indicate that he has some
funds. A job would indicate that the employer probably screened him for hiring. Employment would
indicate regular activity and life style.

The defendant's family will be a contact for
defense counsel. His wife, parents, relatives can
verify his residence and their need of him as wage
earner. They can be references.

Some defendants do not wish to use their employers or family as references when they are in criminal court. They fear the loss of their job or breakup of their home. Defense counsel's search for references for his clients is one of his most demanding chores.

Defendants do not always have the type of contacts easily verified. They may be unemployed, unmarried or separated from family. They become unfavorable risks from lack of a definable background.

If the defense counsel enters a plea of guilty for the defendant, the proceedings are over. The defendant may be paroled under supervision of the Office of Probation. The defendant may receive a suspended sentence and be freed. The defendant may be sentenced to serve time in jail or prison under the supervision of the Department of Correction. For the criminal court, then, the case is closed.

If defense counsel enters a plea of not guilty for the defendant, a new phase in the arraignment proceeding is reached. The plea of not guilty requires the assessment of the likelihood of the defendant's appearance at trial or flight from trial prosecution. This is the third criterion of bailability. The probability of the defendant's appearance or flight is the only statutory criterion of bailability.[34] All the rest are procedural measurements of this statutory requirement. How this probability is assessed will be the substance of further study.

The Bail Setting Phase

Between April 1 and May 25, 1971, the writer personally observed two hundred bail settings in Manhattan Criminal Court. The following patterns emerged in interaction for determination of bail. They are ranked in their frequency of occurrence.

THE BAIL SETTING PHASE

	D	
FAVORABLE DETERMINATION		UNFAVORABLE DETERMINATION
	E	
PRESUMPTION OF INNOCENCE	F	APPARENT NATURE AND STRENGTH OF PROOF
	E	
	N	
	D	
PROBABILITY OF APPEARANCE	A	PROBABILITY OF FLIGHT THE CHARGE THE PENALTY
	N	
	T	
LEGAL FACTORS		LEGAL FACTORS

SOCIAL FACTORS

POSITIVE   NEGATIVE

JOB PATTERN
FAMILY TIES
RESIDENCE
REFERENCE

TABLE II

TABLE III

	Step 1	Step 2	Step 3
Pattern I:	Prosecutor Requests Bail	Defense Accepts Request	Judge Decides
Pattern II:	Prosecutor Requests Bail	Defense Requests Reduction	Judge Decides
Pattern III:	Prosecutor Requests Bail	Judge Objects to Prosecutor	Judge Decides

TABLE IV

Pattern I. Interaction at Bail Setting

Step 1	Step 2	Step 3	% Total
Prosecution Requests Bail	Defense Accepts Request	Judge Concurs	
96/200	96/200	96/200	48%

Pattern I appears in the following sequence after the prosecutor evaluates the nature of the offense and prior record.

Prosecutor: Your Honor, in the case of Mr. X the people ask bail of . . . dollars

Judge: Counselor /For the defense7, bail is to be set at . . . . Is that acceptable to you and your client?

Defense Counsel: Yes, Your Honor.

In this formal interaction the judge's decision is the ratification of a predetermined informal agreement by prosecutor and defense counsel. It may be a low cash bail or a bond which the defendant can obtain. It is for these reasons that defense counsel is ready to

91

agree. This pattern occurred in 96 or 48% of the cases observed.

TABLE V

Pattern I: INTERACTION PATTERNS
                    IN THE COURTROOM

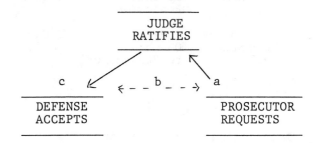

_____   Direct Communication
_ _ _ _ _   Indirect Communication

In Pattern I, it is clear that the courtroom declarations of prosecutor (a) reflect the informal pre-arraignment negotiations with defense. The judge ratifies these negotiations formally at arraignment (b).

It is important to note in Pattern I that defense is not simply a docile receiver of predetermined agreements (c). Defense operates in the formal court-room situation under a number of real handicaps.[35]

First, defense is not a regular member of the establishment. Prosecutor and judge are both public office holders. They regularly work together in roles whose ground rules they have established over their working relationship.

Second, prosecutor and judge develop an institu-tional bond between them in the desire to promote the swift administration of justice. This bond is cemented by shared values in the procedures for dealing with criminal defendants which enable them to work together in court.[36]

Third, defense counsel appears in court in a defensive position. He is there to protect one accused of criminal acts. The power to charge with a crime, the power to ask for stringent conditions of release by the prosecutor, place defense counsel in a suppliant's position. He must bargain as effectively as he can out of court and in to secure the best defense for his client.

The defense lawyer is not an elected or appointed public official. He does not represent "the people" as judge and prosecutor do. The words of the bail request by the prosecutor, "The people ask bail of . . . ." illustrates this phenomenon. Defense counsel, while he may share the value system,[37] background,[38] and education[39] of both judge and prosecutor, is there to represent others whose value system often is quite different.

TABLE VI

Pattern II: INTERACTION AT BAIL SETTING

	Step 1	Step 2	Step 3	$ Total
A	Prosecutor Requests Bail	Defense Requests Reduction to ROR	Judge Decides For Reduction	
	55/200	55/200	40/200	20%
B			Judge Decides Against Reduction	
			15/200	7.5%

Pattern II emerged in the four following ways.

A. Prosecutor: The People ask bail of X dollars, Your Honor.

Defense Counsel: Your Honor, in view of my client's circumstances I ask bail be waived and my client be released on recognizance.

93

Judge: Is that acceptable to the prosecution?

Prosecutor: Yes, Your Honor.

The formula described above reflects an important social problem. The prosecutor never asks for the release of a defendant on his own recognizance (R.O.R.) or zero dollar bail. However, he is willing to agree to it if defense counsel's biographical data on the defendant are favorable.[40] This occurred in forty cases or twenty percent of the observations.

B. Prosecutor: The People ask bail of X dollars, Your Honor.

Defense Counsel: Your Honor, in view of my client's circumstances I ask that bail be waived and my client released on his own recognizance.

Judge: Is that acceptable to the Prosecutor?

Prosecutor: No, Your Honor, it is not.

In fifteen cases, or seven and a half percent, release on recognizance was denied because of prosecution objection (B) to defense motion for reduction. The factors heard in court which prosecution mentioned as basis for their objection include, "The accused has a long history of arrests. . ."; "the accused has committed this offense several times before. . ."; "the accused appears to be without any visible means of support. . ."; "the accused is an addict. . ."; "the accused is an old hand at this sort of thing. . . ."

TABLE VII

Pattern II: INTERACTION AT BAIL SETTING

C	Prosecution Requests Bail	Defense Requests Reduction to 10% Cash	Judge Decides For Reduction	
	35/200	35/200	30/200	15%
D			Judge Decides Against Reduction	
			5/200	2.5%

Pattern II will appear in Form C when, after bail has been requested by prosecution according to the formula which appears in "A," defense will request reduction to "10% cash," that is, 10% of the total amount prosecution requests payable in cash. If prosecution asks for $500 bail, defense will ask for $50 cash bail, knowing defendant can produce it, and because defense counsel knows the correlation between crime category and amounts usually requested as well as the prosecutor. Defense counsel is likely to ask for cash bail rather than release on recognizance in cases where the defendant has a prior record. This would include prostitutes, petty thieves, and similar minor recidivists. These are people who are apt to be jobless, without fixed residence or references. Their biographies are less capable of verification except as a criminal record "yellow sheet." Of 35 requests, 30 were approved and five denied. The denials were in cases of aggravated circumstances such as violence or use of a weapon to which the prosecutor objected to reduction.

TABLE VIII

Pattern II: INTERACTIONS IN THE COURTROOM

Favorable to Defense

In Pattern II A and C, the judge ratifies the request of the defense in court 35% of the time. This was in 70 cases out of 200 observed.

TABLE IX

Patterns II.   INTERACTIONS IN THE COURTROOM

Favorable to Prosecution

B and D

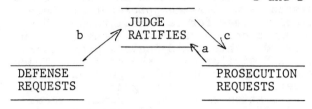

TABLE X

Pattern III: INTERACTION AT BAIL SETTING

	Step 1	Step 2	Step 3	% Total
A	Prosecutor Requests Bail	Judge Objects to Prosecutor	Judge Decides Bail is Too High	
	14/200	14/200	8/200	4%
B			Judge Decides Bail is Too Low[41]	
			6/200	3%

Pattern III emerged with minimal frequency and revealed the flexibility of the system. In spite of any agreement between prosecution and defense counsel and regardless of the usual procedure of requesting a certain bail for a certain offense, the judge can interject immediately on presentation of the charge and the bail request and alter it. In the two hundred cases observed, the judge interjected himself immediately after the prosecution asked for bail in eight cases. He raised the amount without hearing the defense whose objections he denied after he set bail. In these cases the two differing judges gave the

96

following reasons for raising bail: 1)"I have had too
many of your kind /prostitute/ in here today."42   2) "I
have seen you in here too often for this /drunk, abuse
of policeman/." "I wish I could lock all you addicts
up." "The victim may die, bail is denied." "You are
here on several counts, bail is set at $2500," which
was the sum of bail amounts for each offense /prostitute
for assault with weapon/. "This defendant can afford
to pay" /a business man violating the sanitary code
while intoxicated in a subway/.

    In six cases bail was reduced. "Officer, do not
bring me any more of these peddlers. You are released
until /date/ when you must appear before me. If you
stay out of trouble till then your case will be dismissed." Another businessman was released on his own
recognizance by a judge after a display of public
drunkeness, having spent the night in the station
house lockup. His case was postponed for 30 days when
he was to report to the court. In the four remaining
cases, the judge felt the defendants were good risks
without consulting defense counsel and he released them
with a warning to stay out of trouble, return in a
specified number of days to appear before him and their
cases would be dismissed.43

TABLE XI

Pattern III: INTERACTION IN THE COURTROOM
                    THE JUDICIAL PREROGATIVE

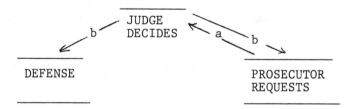

    In the Pattern III scenarios the prosecutor is
overruled by the judge without consulting defense and
for the judge's own reasons as articulated earlier.
These fourteen cases, or 7% of the sample, indicate
a rebuff for the prosecutor. They are decisions made
based on judicial prerogative, that is, the right of
the judge to make a determination as he sees fit

97

according to law.[44]

An analysis of the patterns in bail setting in these two hundred cases reveals:

TABLE XII

	Pattern I	Pattern II	Pattern III	Total
Prosecutor Requests Affirmed	96	20	0	116 58%
Defense Request Affirmed	0	70	0	70 35%
Judge Affirmed			14	14 7%
				200/100%

These patterns indicated: first, the prosecution will try to settle as many cases as possible in pre-arraignment negotiations. The defense actively participates and agrees in these pre-arraignment negotiations. It is rare that defense will surprise prosecution and make a counter-proposal in court once negotiations are settled. However, not being privy to these pre-arraignment conferences, it is impossible to ascertain definitely if any of defense counsel's counter-suggestions were breaches of pre-arraignment negotiations. Some evidence of this may appear when prosecution is adamant in refusing to accede to defense counsel's suggestion for reduced bail. Since it is observed that the judge ratifies the prosecution's request in 58% of all cases, the power of the prosecutor becomes clear. The judge's enunciation of a choice for bail is less a rebuff to the prosecutor, although it may be so construed, than an exercise of the judge's prerogative to be more than a passive role-taker in the arraignment proceedings. It is an assertion of his right to an active role which he may enter upon whenever he sees fit.

What becomes clear in the analysis of these two

hundred cases is that it is to the prosecutor's advantage to settle bail before arraignment. He can offer better bargains, as Newman points out.[45] The bail determination is an appendage to the charge the prosecutor is willing to negotiate. Defense counsel, aware of the working relationships of judge and prosecutor, has to decide whether it is better to take his chances in the pre-arraignment bargain or to bargain in the courtroom.

His reluctance to bargain in the courtroom is rooted in his awareness that the judge wishes to share responsibility for the decisions he makes with the prosecutor. Blumberg notes

> Traditional judicial formulations would require the judge to act as an instrument of the whole community in reviewing the propriety of an accepted lesser plea. But here too. . .judges have abdicated and prefer to ratify the plea negotiated by the district attorney, the defense counsel and sometimes even the police. While the judge may have the right to reject a given plea, he rarely does so.[46]

The bail determination which is part of the plea arrangement is subject to the same informal rules.

The reasons for this are complex to observe and difficult even for the judge to articulate. They include

> . . .reluctance to shoulder the decision-making burden, and an ambivalent attitude towards formal rules and critera which may interfere with his informal relations with . . .court personnel. . . .[47]

The data will show whether or not the judge is "ambivalent towards formal rules and criteria" as Blumberg alleges. It has been the contention of the Vera Institute of Justice[48] and the Legal Aid Society[49] that judicial ambivalence is the result of legislative imprecision in drawing up the procedural laws and the consequently wider latitude available for individual judicial interpretation.

The Judge as Institutional Decision Maker

Introduction

What appears to be a clearcut relationship between the defendant accused of an infraction of the law and the law itself is a relationship that is mediated by others. The chief mediator between the defendant and the law is the judge. It is his decision which will determine the fate of the defendant in the initial stages of the criminal justice process.

The defendant who enters the criminal court to answer a formal complaint does not see the entirety of the institutional system which has placed that judge on that bench before him that day. That institutional system possesses an administrative life of its own which the defendant only glimpses as he proceeds through the processes by which justice is administered.

In 1970 there were twelve judges hearing criminal cases in criminal court. These cases included youthful offenders, adult arraignment - day and night, trial parts for misdemeanors, violations and hearings.

The criminal court branch of the judicial system is considered to be a low-level career line.[50] This is because the type of judicial activity involved is so circumscribed by the volume of cases and procedural rules. There is little opportunity for precedent making, although a judge at arraignment has many options for exercising control over the defendants.

The judge at arraignment is subject to many pressures in his decision making which trial and appeal judges do not face.

The Judge as Decision Maker

The judge in the criminal court is constantly under scrutiny as decision maker. Administrative Judge of the Criminal Court, David Ross, in an interview June 18, 1971, indicated that the backlog of criminal court cases had been reduced in Manhattan from 9,197 on January 1, to 8,461 on April 30, 1971.[51] The judges are under daily observation to clear their calendar and dispose of cases. Abraham Blumberg shows how plea bargaining became a mechanism for disposing of cases.[52]

The plea bargain means entering a plea of guilty at arraignment to a lesser charge or charges with a concomitantly lesser penalty or penalties to avoid standing trial on a more severe charge and in hope of receiving a suspended sentence for cooperating with the court. It affords a high conviction rate to reduced charges at low cost to the court by avoiding continuances, reappearances and the formalities of bail, trial and its attendant legal paper work.[53]

The plea bargain is pertinent to this study insofar as it shows that a plea of guilty takes the defendant out of defendant status and places him in the convicted status. This reduces the number of bail applications. The convicted person is not eligible for pre-trial parole. The defendant's awareness of his own economic circumstances will often prompt him to plead guilty in hope of a suspended sentence since he knows he has not the funds to post bail.

The importance of these considerations to the judge at arraignment goes beyond the economic. First, it allows the convicted person to be given a suspended sentence and placed on probation. This shifts the area of responsibility from the court to the Office of Probation. Second, if the convicted person is given a jail sentence he is shifted to another agency of the criminal justice system, the Department of Correctional Services.

Considering the number of cases brought before the Criminal Court in 1969[54] and 1970,[55] there are not enough trial parts for all the cases to be heard at trial regardless of their status as felonies, misdemeanors or violations. Consider that 100,000 trials by jury would require 1,400,000 jurors. No city could afford the jurors' stipend nor the man-hours lost from employment.

From 1950 through 1971 fewer than 200 cases were tried in Supreme Court annually.

It is at this juncture when the choice is between a plea of guilty or not guilty and its options of detention or pre-trial parole that the adversarial nature of the arraignment interaction between the prosecutor and defense counsel comes to bear. The judge must decide who will be released and who will be detained.

101

VOLUME OF CASES DISPOSED BY TRIAL IN SUPREME COURT

1951 - 1971[56]

Year	Number of Indictments by Grand Jury	Total Disposed By Trial
1951	3217	137
1952	3638	127
1953	3532	131
1954	3934	112
1955	3235	102
1956	3159	114
1957	3524	115
1958	3772	107
1959	4314	104
1960	4750	116
1961	4319	142
1962	4392	162
1963	4997	150
1964	5073	145
1965	5021	147
1966	5203	118
1967	5119	140
1968	5227	151
1969	5567	181
1970	5683	204
1971	5681	207

TABLE XIII

A census conducted by the Federal Government of New York's city and county jails in 1970 and published in January 1971, indicated that 52% of the 17,399 inmates of 75 jails were people awaiting trial.[57] The Manhattan House of Detention, known as the Tombs, held 1,987 inmates on June 9, 1970, or 213% of its 932-person capacity. On June 9, 1971, it held 1,280, or 137% of capacity.[58] More than half of those housed in the Tombs were unable to secure any form of pre-trial release.

On August 10, 1970, the inmates of the Tombs rioted and seized hostages to demonstrate their unresolved grievances.[59]

The judge is pressured to be a good courtroom administrator.

A new system of punishments for
excessive delays in processing cases for
trial in the city's Criminal Court . . .
is to start March 1 in the experimental
Master All Purpose (MAP) project. The
project itself is a new venture begun
Feb. 1 in the New York County with a
Federal grant under the Safe Streets Act.

The MAP program provides for a
conference, after arraignment, in which
the defendant, defense counsel and
prosecutor discuss with a judge what the
defendant's next move might be - a request
for a hearing or a possible plea of guilt,
as examples. No witnesses are called to
attend this first post-arraignment appearance.

May Become Citywide

Judge Ross's new sanctions program is
to be considered for the entire citywide
Criminal Court system if it works well in
the MAP program in reducing excessive
adjournments. The heavily burdened court
handles at least preliminary stages of the
several hundred thousand criminal cases in
the city each year, and disposes of misdemeanors while referring felonies to
Supreme Court.

The experimental effort will allow no
more than two adjournments, and will impose
sanctions for any further delay or for late-
ness and non-appearance that lacks a reasonable excuse.

The sanctions include dismissal for
lack of prosecution, imposition of costs,
fixing or revoking of bail and immediate
hearing or trial. Judge Ross said studies
had shown that prosecutors had been as
responsible as defendants for delays.60

The judge will note the reported increase in
crimes demonstrated before him as an increased flow
of defendants.

The city's rate of reported crimes rose 4.7% in the first 11 months of 1970 over the corresponding period in 1969, the Police Department reported yesterday in an analysis of seven categories of major crimes.

The number of reported crimes in all categories rose from 439,502 in the first 11 months of 1969 to 471,819 in the corresponding period last year, an increase of 7.4 percent.

Muggings, which involve force, and robberies rose by 23.5 percent, from 53,915 cases in the 11-month period of 1969 to 66,585 in the comparable period last year.

During the same periods the number of burglaries rose from 156,522 in 1969 to 165,828 in 1970, an increase of 5.9 percent.

A breakdown of other statistics comparing the first 11 months of 1969 and 1970 showed the following:

A 7.8 percent increase in murder and non-negligent manslaughter, from 954 cases to 1,028 cases.

An increase of 0.9 percent in the number of forcible rapes, from 1,958 cases to 1,975 cases.

A 4.6 percent increase in assaults, from 27,619 cases to 28,894 cases.

A 1.7 percent increase in larcenies - the theft of $50 or more - from 119,225 cases to 121,201 cases.

An increase of 8.8 percent in auto thefts, from 79,309 cases to 86,308 cases.[61]

    The Criminal Justice Coordinating Council stated, "The post-arrest process has received inadequate attention in the budgeting process."[62] A look at the 1970-71 criminal justice budget, which covers the period of our study, reveals that only 1.5% of a total budget of $843,208,910 was allocated to prosecution and defense of offenders.[63]

The chart in Appendix A indicates the budgeting allotments. These allotments demonstrate the priorities of the city in the field of criminal justice.

It is the judge in the criminal court who must work in the environment these funds provide. In 1969, 91,415 adult arrest cases were processed through Manhattan Criminal Court alone.[64] With a budget of $8,966,309 or 1.1% of total for the entire city to prosecute nearly one quarter million defendants, it amounts to $35.89 per defendant from docketing and first interview by a prosecutor, arraignment, continuance, trial and disposition.

The sum of $4,000,000 is allocated for defense of offenders. This sum covers the cost of counsel for the indigent as furnished by the Legal Aid Society and other public defender groups. If one considers only half of all defendants as eligible for legal assistance, it amounts to $32 to see a case through to its conclusion with all costs such as telephone calls, legal documents and transcripts allocated from this sum.

Because of these facts, will the judge accept guilty pleas and pleas to reduced charges, or will he accept pleas of not guilty? If he accepts pleas of not guilty, will he release those so accused pending trial in the face of growing public concern over increased crime, or will he detain defendants in conditions which are admittedly substandard?

The decision the judge makes in accepting a plea of not guilty involves his affirmation of the legal presumption of innocence unless and until proven guilty. The presumption of innocence favors release before trial on application for bail which the U.S. Constitution mandates shall not be excessive. The right to bail is stipulated in the New York State Constitution, Article 1, Section 5 in the same form as the U.S. Constitution. This constitutional provision has been regulated by The Code of Criminal Procedure and The Criminal Procedure Law of 1971.

The pressures on the judge in decision making are complex. It is not simply to judge whether the defendant accused of a crime has broken a particular law

or laws. The pressure to clear the calendar, the
pressure to keep cases moving, the pressure to keep
costs low, the pressure to be a good administrator in
his courtroom, all function in the judicial decision
making process. "Due process" becomes part of the
institutional program of the court. The judge becomes
part of a system maintenance procedure. Rationality
and discretion remain dependent upon the amount of
information available to the judge. That information
is frequently incomplete and the judge must fall back
upon precedent for decision so that the entire system
may continue to function. If decisions were not
rendered until all the facts were presented in court,
as is the case with trials, then no modality for control of defendants could be utilized until the entire
system acquired more complete and balanced data gathering machinery. In the next two chapters decision
making varieties when factors such as the nature of the
offense, social and pecuniary circumstances are held
constant will be examined. The form of control of the
defendant does not result from a consistent application
of the procedural criteria of bailability.

This long-standing problem has remained unresolved
as the court chose to leave the application of the
criteria of bailability to a minor court official known
as the bail bondsman. The bondsman has established
his own precedents for obtaining the release of those
eligible for bail. Assets in some form have been the
prerequisite.

The Bail Bondsman

Introduction

The pledge of wealth in some form became in the
19th century the standard rule of adequacy in a bail
decision in the United States. This was due in large
measure to the increasing mobility of the American
population. Increasingly transient populations allowed
for people to be increasingly anonymous in their
community. Thus, it would be less likely for a defendant to be released to someone who truly knew him
and was willing to risk being a personal surety. This
phenomenon is very well delineated in an article by
George Pierson, entitled "A Restless Temper. . ."[66] in
which he examines Alexis de Tocqueville's analysis of
American mobility in light of the 20th century phenomena
of mass transportation and highway systems. Thus,

those without resources, even if possessed of social organization such as family, and references such as union membership, if without funds were unable to secure release. The movement of bail reform in the 1960s has been to shift the power base to a more balanced relationship, at least theoretically.[67]

The United States developed the phenomenon of the bail bondsman, an agent who provides an insurance company surety bond for persons who find themselves accused of a crime. The bondsman's surety has been seen as the safest form of pledge by the Court. The bondsman's surety bond has converted all forms of collateral into funds payable to the court should the defendant fail to appear. The bond pledged is released to the insurer when the defendant appears for trial.

The Bondsman's Formal Role

Bail bondsmen are minor court officials. They are certified agents of insurance companies licensed to write bail bonds by the New York State Department of Insurance. As the insurer of the defendant, bondsmen have acquired responsibility for the person of the defendant.

> What does it cost a judge if he paroles some guy and the guy don't show? Henry asks. Judges don't care. The D.A.'s office don't care. But when I write a bond, I have to really check a guy out. Roots in the community, collateral, family, background, the works. With me, it costs money if some guy I write for turns out to be a lamster. I'm involved, see?

> Despite his involvement, Henry concedes that his forfeitures have gone up during the past two years at an alarming rate. Every bond is a hazard these days, Henry says. A bondsman is a kind of gambler.[68]

The defendant's failure to appear when on bail in addition to being a crime requires the surety to forfeit the face value of the bond. Insurers over the years have developed their own perceptual shorthand for evaluating applicants for bail bonds.[69]

I don't understand people who take a fall
for a cause, he says. Give me a bookmaker
any day. He does what he does for money.
This I understand.

    . . .bondsmen insist on collateral from their
clients before they write a bond. Most bondsmen can read collateral better than a banker
or credit manager. The amount varies from
bondsman to bondsman. It can be as little
as 20 percent on a good risk, such as an
established bookmaker, to 100 percent on a
bad risk, like a transient stickup man.
Power men are very particular about what they
accept as collateral. Bank books are considered the best bets, with deeds to property
and titles to automobiles running a close
second. Some take stocks and bonds. A few
regard insurance policies and jewelry as
tolerable security. At times, even wedding
rings and sets of false teeth have been
utilized as collateral. But when it comes to
his commission, the power man will accept
only hard currency.

    The premiums for bail bonds are regulated by
the State Insurance Department and run 5
percent on the first thousand dollars, 4
percent on the second thousand and 3 percent
on each thousand after that.[70]

    Under The Code of Criminal Procedure when the
choice was between a bail bond or jail, that one free
phone call often went to a bondsman. Bondsmen's phone
numbers were posted in interview rooms adjacent to
arraignment court.

    The bondsman had become a powerful man, able to
secure the release or detention of the defendant. In
some cases this powerful position has led to corruption
among bondsmen, as the 1971 investigation of bondsmen
by District Attorney Hogan's Office in Manhattan noted.

    According to Asst. District Attorneys
    Jeffrey Hoffman and Michael Berne, the
    fraud worked this way:

    Under normal bonding procedures, a
    defendant deposits with a bondsman
    cash or collateral - jewels, a deed,
    a car ownership - equal in value to

his bail. He also pays the bondsman a
fee ($25 on the first $500; $20 on each
additional $500) for his services.

Should the defendant jump bail, the bondsman is responsible for converting the
collateral into cash and paying the court,
which turns the money over to the city.

Yesterday's indictment charges that . . .
waived the collateral on 245 defendants in
return for under-the-table payments.

The payments averaged $50 for each $1,000
in bail. Therefore, for $95 ($50 under-
the-table and $45 in bonding fee) a de-
fendant could escape putting up the small
sum to lose, the indictment charges, the
defendants chose to jump bail.[71]

The Manhattan grand jury released an indictment in
this case which listed 444 counts charging the bondsmen and their co-conspirators with defrauding the city
of forfeited bonds.[72]

The Bondsman's Informal Role

In some cases of failure to appear, bonds have not
been collected because bondsmen have established
connections within the court system to cover this
eventuality. Perhaps one of the most difficult to
prove and corruptive of practices has been "steering."
This is a process whereby certain bondsmen are favored
by a judge who recommends defendants to the select
bondsman. The fees collected for the writing of bond
for the defendants so recommended are split between
bondsman and judge. Similar "steering" practices are
possible with lawyers.[73] However unappealing the
corruptive elements of the bondsmen's world may appear,
he filled a need over a period of years for both the
court and defendants.

FOOTNOTES

1. Max Weber on Law in Economy and Society, pp. 307-308, 316, 318.

2. Paul A. Freund, On Law and Justice. Cambridge: The Belknap Press, 1968, p. 63.

3. Benjamin N. Cardozo, The Nature of the Judicial Process. New Haven: Yale University Press, 1921, Chapter 3. See also Alexander and Staub, The Criminal, The Judge and The Public, 1931.

4. Jack P. Gibbs, "The Sociology of Law and Normative Phenomena," American Sociological Review, Vol. 31, June 1966, p. 320.

5. "Administration of Bail in New York City," University of Pennsylvania Law Review, pp. 695-696, note 11.

6. Code of Criminal Procedure, Vol. 66, Section 552, McKinney's Consolidated Laws of New York, Brooklyn, N.Y.: Edward Thompson, 1968 ed.

7. Wolfgang Friedman, "Limits of Judicial Lawmaking and Prospective Overruling." Modern Law Review, Vol. 29, No. 6. November 1966.

8. Amitai Etzioni, "Two Approaches to Organizational Analysis: A Critique and a Suggestion." Administrative Science Quarterly, September 1960, pp. 257-78.

9. Freund, op. cit., p. 68.

10. Ibid., p. 69.

11. John Rawls, A Theory of Justice. Cambridge: The Harvard University Press (Belknap), 1972.

12. Criminal Procedure Law, Section 1:20.10.

13. Ibid., Section 530.20.

14. Ibid., Section 500.10.10.

15. Ibid., Section 500.10.13.

16. "Judge Supported on Prostitution." The New York Times, Sunday, August 1, 1971.

17. Wilfred Rumble, Jr., "Legal Realism, Sociological Jurisprudence and Mr. Justice Holmes." Journal of the History of Ideas, Vol. XXVI, October-December 1965, pp. 547-66.

18. Bail and Summons: 1965, p. 93. See also Schaffer, "The Problem of Overcrowding. . ." p. 3, and "Bail and Parole Jumping in Manhattan in 1967," pp. 47-48. P. Wald, "Pre-trial Detention. . ." p. 631.

19. "A Study of the Administration of Bail in New York City," p. 693f. See also note 18.

20. Leslie T. Wilkins, Social Deviance. New Jersey: Prentice Hall, Inc., 1964, pp. 18-25.

21. Ibid., p. 18.

22. Criminal Procedure Law, Section 1.20.6.

23. Ibid., Section 1.20.7 and 8.

24. Ibid., Section 1.20.9

25. Frederic Suffet, "Bail Setting: A Study of Courtroom Interaction." New York: The Vera Institute of Justice (reprint) 1965, p. 319 and p. 323.

26. Code of Criminal Procedure, Section 550, case note 2.

27. Donald Newman, "Pleading Guilty for Consideration: A Study in Bargain Justice." Journal of Criminal Law, Criminology and Police Science, 46 (March-April 1956), pp. 780-790.

28. Blumberg, op. cit., p. 133.

29. Ibid., p. 57.

30. Schaffer, op. cit., pp. 4-8.

31. Suffet, op. cit., p. 320.

32. Blumberg, op. cit., Table 2, p. 30, and Table 6, p. 92.

33. See standard report of the search for criminal record.

34. Penal Law, Vol. 39, Sections 100-219 in McKinney's Consolidated Laws of New York, Brooklyn, N.Y.: Edward Thompson, 1968 ed.

35. Sudnow, "Normal Crimes: Sociological Features of the Penal Code in a Public Defender Office," Social Problems 12 (Winter 1965), pp. 255-76.

36. Blumberg, op. cit., Chapter 5, pp. 97-99.

37. Jerome Carlin, Lawyer's Ethics. New York: Russell Sage Foundation, 1966.

38. F.S.C. Northrop, The Complexity of Legal and Ethical Experience. Boston: Little Brown, 1959.

39. Blumberg, op. cit., Chapter 5.

40. See Table II, Ideal Bail Risk Profile, Chapter 1, p. 22.

41. "Judge Supported on Prostitution," The New York Times, August 1, 1971.

42. See note 41, above.

43. Author's courtroom observations, April, May 1971.

44. Code of Criminal Procedure, Section 550, case note 2.

45. Donald J. Newman, "Pleading Guilty for Considerations: A Study of Bargain Justice," Journal of Criminal Law, Criminology and Police Science, 46 (March-April 1956), pp. 780-790.

46. Blumberg, op. cit., p. 131.

47. Ibid., p. 130.

48. Ares, Rankin & Sturz, "The Manhattan Bail Project. . .," pp. 697ff.

49. Legal Aid Study, pp. 27-30. See Chapter I, p. 4. See also Daniel J. Freed and Patricia Wald, Bail in the United States, Washington, D.C.: The National Conference on Bail and Criminal Justice, 1965.

50. Blumberg, op. cit., p. 120.

51. Interview with Judge David Ross, June 18, 1971.

52. Blumberg, op. cit., pp. 131-136.

53. See Table I, above.

54. Flow of Arrested Defendants. . ., pp. 18-20.

55. Ibid., p. 21.

56. Annual Report, City Magistrates' Courts, City of New York, 1951-1962, and Annual Report, Criminal Court, New York City, 1963-71.

   Prior to 1962 the Supreme Court was a court of general jurisdiction according to the New York City Criminal Courts Act, Section 22. It rarely exercised criminal jurisdiction. Court of Special Sessions had jurisdiction over misdemeanors. In New York County felonies were tried in the Court of General Sessions, which is now the Supreme Court, by the 1962 reorganization.

57. "Jail Census Finds 52% Not Convicted." The New York Times, January 1, 1971.

   Jails are for people detained before trial and for those convicted of misdemeanor and violation category crimes with sentences less than one year.

58. See note 51.

59. "Text of Inmate Grievances," The New York Times, August 11, 1971. See Part One.

60. "New Penalties for Court Delays Are Announced." The New York Times, February 21, 1971.

61. "Increase of 7.4% in Major Crimes Reported by City," The New York Times, January 8, 1971.

62. Report of the Mayor's Criminal Justice Coordinating Council, 1972 (mimeo), p. 70.

63. Ibid., p. 70.

64. Flow of Arrested Defendants. . ., p. 24.

65. "Text of Judge Stanley Fuld's Statement on the Courts," New York Times, October 18, 1970.

66. George Pierson, "A Restless Temper. . . ." The American Historical Review, Vol. LXIX, No. 4, July 1964, pp. 969-989.

67. Fred Graham, The Self-Inflicted Wound. New York: The Macmillan Co., 1970, Chapter 1.

68. "Hard Times on Bail Bond Row," p. 44, vide fn. 67, Chapter I.

69. See any standard Bail Bond Form.

70. "Hard Times on Bail Bond Row," p. 44.

71. "Bail Men May Face DA Probe." The New York Post, October 26, 1971.

72. Ibid., p. 3.

73. "Bail Setting: A Study of Courtroom Interaction," p. 319.

CHAPTER IV

TYPES OF BAIL AND THE SOCIAL
CIRCUMSTANCES OF THE DEFENDANTS

Introduction: The Nature and Method of the Study

This study was undertaken to analyze the relationship between the bail condition and the social circumstances of the defendants to demonstrate how the type
of bail affects the defendants in an immediate and
causal way. The study sampled closed case files of 878
individuals who were all represented by counsel associated with Manhattan Criminal or the Supreme Court
branches of the Legal Aid Society. All those in the
sample population had gone through the bail-setting
process. Thirty-eight percent of those in the sample
population were not held in jail pending the outcome of
their case. Whether this was due to the social circumstances of the defendant or whether the defendant was
able to raise enough funds to make bail will be examined
in Chapters V and VI. In this chapter we will examine
the bail groupings by amount and their relationship to
what we will establish as the social circumstances of
the defendant. These social circumstances include age,
marital status, number of dependants and residence only.

This chapter will show the following results: 1)
Age was not a significant factor in the determination
of bail. 2) The marital status of defendants was not
a significant factor in the determination of bail.
3) The number of dependents of the defendant was not
significant in the determination of bail.

Certain consequences were manifest as a result of
these observations. The bail system did not take into
consideration factors which are essentially non-economic.
The bail system was required by law to consider factors
which are non-economic. The bail system as it operated
in New York County denied a person who is detained in
lieu of financial bail equal protection of the laws because it denied to him the opportunity for treatment
equal to a person whose social circumstances were iden-
tical to his in every other circumstance aside from
wealth. This was a constitutionally impermissilbe basis
for differentiation. This constitutional question was
examined in Chapter I.

The 878 closed cases from the files of the Legal
Aid Society chosen for this study permitted multi-
variate analysis of bail. The vast majority of the
cases were ultimately disposed of in Manhattan Criminal
Court. One out of every 14 cases, however, reached
final disposition in the Supreme Court in Manhattan.
This ratio reflected the ratio between Criminal and
Supreme Court cases as handled by the Legal Aid Society

in their Manhattan office over the last several years. The 878 cases sampled were representative numerically of the class of parties called adult males charged with a crime in Manhattan whose cases have involved some form of bail or release decision, and who have been represented at least to the disposition stage by a member of the Legal Aid Society's staff.

The people in the sample population have generally been charged with serious offenses: 55% were charged with felonies; some, 7%, with categories of offenses which, depending upon the proof, might be felonies or misdemeanors; and the rest, 38% with misdemeanors.

Of the 878 people whose cases were sampled, 29% were released on their own recognizance at the time of their arraignment in Criminal Court. A like percentage, 32% were given bail of $500 or less. For another 15% of the people bail was set at $1,000. Bail of more than $1,000 was set in 24% of the cases.

In all but 3% of the sample cases, when bail was set it was fixed in multiples of $500. In the remaining 3% of the cases bail was set at less than $500. In three-quarters of all cases in which bail was set, it was set at either $500, $1,000 or $2,500. Furthermore, the data indicating the amount of time spent in fixing bail are consistent with the amount of time spent in the arraignment and bail-setting process for the cases which are studied in this chapter. These observations indicate that there is not adequate time provided for individual consideration of the social circumstances of each defendant which would be appropriate to the bail-setting process.

In order to carry out multivariate analysis with as many as four or five variables examined simultaneously, a sample of at least 800 cases was necessary. The total population in the sample was drawn from closed files for the New York office of the Legal Aid Society as of December 15, 1971. A case is placed in the Society's closed files when there has been a final disposition of the charges at the trial court level, and no further proceedings remain to be taken. Of the 878 cases in the sample, 800 were disposed of in Criminal Court, and the remainder were treated in Supreme Court. Certain categories of cases were excluded from the sample taken: 1) Anyone other than adult males. Since it was necessary to examine jail records in order to obtain certain data, it would be difficult to secure the records for many women because the Women's House of Detention in Manhattan had recently closed. 2) Anyone whose case was disposed of at arraignment was excluded. This would include all cases of plea bargaining in which the defendant pleaded guilty or had his case dismissed when he first came to court, and therefore was not included in the bail-setting process. 3) Any case in which there was an incomplete trial record. Incomplete trials would be those which lacked one of the following documents: the complaint; a report to the court from the Department of Probation's Bureau of Release on Recognizance, known as the ROR Report; a history of the accused's prior offenses, which is known as the Yellow Sheet, supplied by the Bureau of Criminal Investigation; the cover sheet prepared in court at the arraignment and studied and annotated by the Society's attorneys who handle the case. Since one purpose of this study was to analyze the data which the court had before it when bail was set or when release was ordered, and since in many cases it was impossible to ascertain whether the absence of any given document was due to its having been lost or not provided in the first place, those cases with missing documents were excluded. Other cases where the Legal Aid Society was replaced by private counsel before the final disposition were excluded.

The time period studied for the Criminal Court cases was based on arraignments which took place during the months of April, May and June of 1971. By selecting arraignment cases which would be at least six months to nine months old from the records of Criminal Court, it was felt that an appropriate balance had been achieved among three considerations: first, the need for data at least as detailed as that currently used by the courts in setting bail; second, the need for data as complete as possible; third, the need to allow a sufficient time period after arraignment so that cases could be closed, that is, disposed of. It is important to note that this study does exclude cases with very long pre-trial detention periods which are frequently publicized. The case files were selected on a random basis in the following manner. The Society's closed files are numbered consecutively throughout the year. Thus, with both Criminal and Supreme Court cases, files were drawn originally on the basis of the last digit of their Society-assigned file number. These were then screened to exclude those cases which were considered inapplicable for the study.

118

Then all cases ending with a different last digit during this same period were pulled from the files, and the same selection process was repeated until a sample population attained the size of approximately 900 cases.

The information which is contained in the Society's files was transferred from the files on to data sheets written in the form of a questionnaire. On this data sheet were included all items which were regarded as relevant variables for the study. These would include the background characteristics of the accused, the nature of the charge, his prior record, whether bail was set, in what amount, and whether it was posted. The data were pretested by Legal Aid attorneys and revisions made where necessary. The information on the data sheets was transferred to IBM data-processing cards. A key-punch operation was performed at the Academic Computer Center of New York University. The data on the IBM cards were then analyzed by New York University's Academic Computer Center program called "BMD-08D" under the supervision of Mr. David Sternberg of the Academic Computer Center.

The analysis proceeded in several stages. First, tabulations on a frequency of distribution of each item on the questionnaire were examined after they had been printed. Then basic true variable analysis was performed. These variables included the bail determination, the amount of bail, the age, marital status of defendants. All variables were examined while holding the crime category constant and several other variables in series. The next step entailed an examination of selected two- and three-variable relationships. The purpose of such an examination is to determine whether a relationship is in fact a causal one or whether that relationship is due to some other factor, such as a test factor.[1]

In this study there is an observed relationship between the pretrial bail choice and the social circumstances of the defendants. This relationship is essentially negative. It is examined while numerous test variables were administered. Each variable failed to explain the relationship, indicating that it is causal in the sense that it is operating to the detriment of the defendant. This is the logic underlying the multivariate analysis and set forth in the data that follow on a step-by-step basis.

Bail Groupings in General by Amount

The 878 cases studied fell into three classifications of conditional release: bail bond, cash bail, or release on recognizance. Traditionally these have been seen in monetary terms, that is, by the amount of money posted for release, or the face value of the bail bond. Release on recognizance is that form of pretrial parole in which the defendant is permitted his liberty without having to post any form of collateral other than his verbal agreement to appear when required.[2] This form has been officially used only since 1964.[3] All three forms of pretrial parole require that defendants meet the criteria for bailability of the code.[4] These criteria have been discussed in Chapter III.

The central question will be how are the "social circumstances" of the defendant weighed in the determination of pretrial parole as required by law. The factors of "social circumstances" which came into play were those which appear on the required forms for the arraignment of a criminal case.[5] These factors were: age, marital status, family ties or dependents, residence. For purposes of analysis income and employment were examined under the heading of "economic circumstances" in the evaluation of bailability as the Code stipulates. These factors will be analyzed in Chapter V.[6]

First how the defendants in the sample population actually were released, the outcome of the arraignment proceeding, was examined.

There were 29.3% (257) released on recognizance, which is generally called "ROR," while 70.3% (621) had to find other alternatives. For this remainder the choices appeared as bail bond or cash bail. Table II shows the actual bail bond amounts in relation to the age of the defendants and the category of crime with which they have been charged.[7]

FORMS OF CONDITIONAL RELEASE

TYPE OF PRE-TRIAL PAROLE	NUMBER RELEASED	NUMBER DETAINED	ROW TOTAL	ROW %
Release on Recognizance	257	0	257	29.3%
Bail Bond	36	430	446*	53.1%
Cash Bail	43	106	149	16.8%
Column Total Number	366	536	872	
Total %	38.6%	60.7%	99.3%	

*There are six cases whose form of release is unknown.

TABLE I

121

ACTUAL BAIL BOND HELD CONSTANT BY AMOUNT
MEASURED AGAINST AGE AND CRIME CATEGORY

AGE	Crime Category	1-99	100-250	251-500	501-1000	1001 to 2500	2501 to 5000	Other	Row Total
21-30	1	4		53	21	18	15	3	114
	2	1		20	23	25	7	4	80
	3	1		55	2	25		4	87
31-40	1	1		34	8	8	7		58
	2			11	6	14	4		35
	3			20	1	8	8		37
41-50	1			8		6			14
	2			5		4	2	1	12
	3		8	6	4	3	2		23
51-over	1	1		3	1				5
	2					2			2
	3					2	1	2	5
COLUMN TOTAL		8	8	215	66	115	46	14	472
									878 53% of all cases

TABLE II

Three hundred ninety six out of 472 (83%) bail bonds fall into the range of $251 - $2500. Two hundred eighty one out of 472 (59%) bonds were written for those between 21 and 30 years of age, regardless of crime category. The highest incidence of arraignment is also in this age category of 21 to 30. Crime category one accounted for 191 (41%) of all bond offenses cases regardless of age. Category three ranked second with 152 cases (32%), and category two accounts for 129 cases (28%) of all bond cases. This table will be analyzed for the social factors further on in the text. The infrequency of bail bond below $250 was related to the cash bail option which allowed a defendant to post 10% of the full value of the bail bond, if possible, to obtain pretail release. It was worth noting that 15 bonds were issued under $250, seven being for sums less than $100.

Table III shows the frequency of distribution of the cash bail option measured by age and crime category.

ACTUAL CASH BAIL HELD CONSTANT BY AMOUNT
MEASURED AGAINST AGE AND CRIME CATEGORY

AGE	Crime Category	1-50	51-100	100-500	Other	Row Total
21-30	1	13	23	11		47
	2	1	4	4		9
	3	13	16	6		35
31-40	1	5	7	6	1	19
	2	2		3		5
	3	5	8	3		16
41-50	1	1	4			5
	2	3		2		5
	3	1	2			3
51-over	1	1	2	1		4
	2					
	3		1			1
COLUMN TOTAL		45	67	36	1	149

TABLE III

16.8% of all cases

123

Table III indicates, as does Table II, that the highest incidences of bail were in the middle range amount of $51 - $100, 67 out of 149 (44.9%). The highest incidences of cash bail were for those between 21 and 30 years of age, 91 out of 149 (60.9%). There was a clear pattern of high incidence of arraignment and bail among the youngest adults with the frequency of arraignment and bail decreasing with the age of the defendants.

Age, Crime Category and Type of Pretrial Parole

Table IV will show how all three forms of pretrial release compare in relation to age and crime category.

ALL FORMS OF PRE-TRIAL RELEASE

Age	Crime Category	Bail Bond	Cash Bail	ROR*	Total	Row &%	
21-30	1	114	47	121	282	32.1	
	2	80	9	17	106	12.0	61.0%
	3	87	35	26	148	16.9	
31-40	1	58	19	39	116	13.2	
	2	35	5	6	46	5.2	24.3%
	3	37	16	7	60	5.9	
41-50	1	14	5	17	36		
	2	12	5	2	19		
	3	23	3	3	29		
51-60	1	4	2	9	15		
	2	2		2	4		
	3	4	1	4	9		
61-over	1	1	2	4	7		
	2						
	3	1			1		
Column %		53.9%	16.8%	29.3%	100%		
Column Total		472	149	257	878		

*ROR = ZERO DOLLARS, thus it has no numerical range.

TABLE IV

Table IV shows the distribution of bail alternatives. It was important to keep in mind that only
the ROR category indicates the total who were actually
released, where money was not a factor. Of those
eligible for release on bond or cash bail, only a
percentage were able to obtain release as will be seen
in Parts Three and Four. This required the reiteration
of the question: what social factors, if any, enter the
determination of pretrial release, and how were they
employed?

The following conclusions were clear on the
basis of the data described. First, more defendants
were required to post bail, cash or bond, than were
released on recognizance in the under-50 years of age
group, regardless of offense, while in the over-50 age
group the bail or "ROR" release ratio was equal.
Second, the fact that 85.3% of all arraignments in the
sample were for adult defendants under 40 years of age,
with 61% of all arraignments for those under 30
indicates that while there was a higher number of
arraignments for younger men, their chances of obtaining release on recognizance were less than 1 in 2,
regardless of category of offense.

AGE AND RELEASE RATIO
(21 - 40 AGE GROUP)
IN RELATION TO CRIME CATEGORY

AGE	CRIME CATEGORY	ALL BAIL	ROR	TOTAL ROW
21-30	1	161	121	282
	2	89	17	106
	3	122	26	148
COLUMN TOTAL		372	164	536
31-40	1	77	39	116
	2	40	6	46
	3	53	7	60
		170	52	222

TABLE V

125

Table V indicates that age was not a significant factor in weighing the choice of pretrial release. There was no significant discrepancy in the ratio of release types at any age level. This indicated that the age of the defendant was not a major consideration in the determination of pretrial release. Table VI took the age and crime category one relationship which contains 51.6% of all cases.

AGE AND RELEASE ON RECOGNIZANCE IN CRIME CATEGORY ONE

RELEASE	21-30	31-40	41-50	51-60	61-over	ROW TOTAL
ROR	121	39	17	9	4	190
ALL BAIL	158*	77	19	6	3	263
COLUMN TOTAL	279*	116	36	15	7	453

* 3 dispositions unknown

TABLE VI

Table VI shows that men over 50 had a slightly greater chance of release on recognizance than younger men in crime category one, which includes offenses such as homicides, sex crimes, assault, arson and burglary. The difference has to lie in the evaluation of some other factor than age.

Table VII shows that the greater number of defendants are between 21 and 30, regardless of offense. This preponderance of younger people allows the judge some flexibility in dealing with other age groups. However, such flexibility does not appear except in the few instances shown above in Table VI.

AGE AND CRIME CATEGORY

Crime Category Penal Code	21-30	31-over	Row Total
1. 100.00 - 150.05	282	174	456
2. 150.10 - 200.05	106	69	175
3. 200.10 - 270.15	148	99	247
COLUMN TOTAL	536	342	878

TABLE VII

The evidence from Tables V, VI and VII indicated: 1) holding the age of defendants constant, the chance of obtaining release on recognizance are less than 2 to 1; 2) holding the crime category constant, the age of the defendant does not emerge as significant in determining release. In the sections that follow, the factors of marital status, dependants and residence will be analyzed to assess their relation to the crime category and type of release.

Marital Status, Crime Category and Pretrial Release

The possible categories of marital relationship which can be examined include: single, widower, divorced, licensed marriage and common-law marriage. Using the same classification of crime category, the forms of release will be analyzed.

Table VIII shows that the greatest number of cases fall into the categories of single and married, regardless of crime category. For the other categories, bail bond is the dominant form. Where marital status is unknown (4%), defendants had to post bond on a ratio better than 3 to 1. Widowers formed a population of four (.45%) in the study; two had to post bond, one was ROR'd and one had a cash bail option. Common-law marriages numbered eight in this sample (.97%) and had to post bond in 7 out of 10 cases; two were ROR'd and one had a cash option.

127

FORMS OF RELEASE: A GENERAL VIEW
BY MARITAL STATUS AND CRIME CATEGORY

Marital Status	Crime Category	Bail Bond	Cash Bail	ROR	Row Total
Unknown	1	13	3	3	19
	2	3	1		4
	3	11	1		12
Single	1	126	46	107	279
	2	86	13	15	114
	3	100	40	22	162
Widower	1	1	1	1	3
	2				
	3	1			1
Divorced	1	4	1	6	11
	2	6		1	7
	3	2			2
Married	1	46	24	72	142
	2	33	5	10	48
	3	33	13	18	64
Common Law	1	1		1	2
	2	1		1	2
	3	5	1		6
		472	149	257	878

TABLE VIII

MARITAL STATUS, CRIME CATEGORY AND CASH BAIL AMOUNT

Marital Status	Crime Category	Bond	Cash Bail			ROR $0	Row Sub-Total	Total
			$1-50	51-100	101-500			
Single	1	126	11	20	15*	107	268	
	2	86	3	4	6	15	114	555
	3	100	14	10	6	22	162	
Married	1	46	7	14	3	72	142	
	2	33	2		3	10	48	254
	3	33	4	6	3	18	64	
COLUMN TOTAL		424	41	64	36	244		809 / 878

* One case of each bail higher than $500.

TABLE IX

129

Table IX highlights the categories of pretrial release relative to personal status, "married" or "single," with crime category held constant and cash bail ranges indicated. It is significant that neither married men nor single men have a high incidence of release on cash bail. The principal options are bond or ROR.

The table reveals that twice as many single men are arraigned as married men in this sample, 555 to 254. For single men in crime category one, their chances of being ROR'd or posting a bail bond are almost equivalent, 126:107. Forty-six men were able to arrange for cash bail. These figures would indicate that the "single state" is not a weighty factor in release before trial. Single men in crime categories two and three seem to be adversely affected by their "singleness." Married men in crime category one are ROR'd more frequently than required to post bail, 46 to 27. However, married men in crime categories two and three show proportionally more adverse effect than single men in their eligibility for pretrial release. Cash bail becomes an option for only 12%. Personal status as "married" or "single" shows these clear relationships in light of the cash bail option:

1) Married men in crime category one are ROR'd or bailed with equal frequency, 72:70. Thus, marital status in crime category one is not a significant factor.

2) Personal status as "married" or "single" in crime categories two and three is a negative factor. It does not contribute anything to the positive release of defendants considering that it is financially more difficult or a hardship to post a bond than 10% of the face value of a bond as cash bail, or be released on recognizance.

Defendants' Dependents, Crime Category and Pretrial Release

It may be suggested that defendants' marital status as such is not relevant, but the presence of dependents in, or associated with the household, such as children or the elderly, is a factor. This factor will now be examined.

DEFENDANTS' DEPENDENTS, CRIME CATEGORY
AND ·PRETRIAL RELEASE

Dependents	Crime Category	Yes ROR	No ROR-But	Bail	Total	
Unknown	1		7			
	2		7			
	3		5			19
Yes	1	45	49		94	
	2	8	25		33	182
	3	11	44		55	
No	1	107	172		279	
	2	18	91		119	551
	3	23	130		153	
Not Applicable	1	38	35		73	
	2	1	29		30	136
	3	6	27		33	
COLUMN TOTAL		257	621		878	

TABLE X

Dependents

Table XI examined the relation between those released on recognizance and those held for bail according to the presence of dependents, for whom they were responsible, with crime category held constant. Such dependents included children, wife, parents. While there were 15 defendants in Group A whose family relations in terms of dependents were unknown, 859 respondents answered categorically. In this table there were no controls for age, marital status and dependents combined; that will be done later. Here the analysis was simply to establish any direct correlation between type of release and dependents.

DEFENDANTS' DEPENDENTS AND ROR

Group	Dependents For Whom Responsible	Crime Category	Release on Recognizance Yes	No	Row Total
A	Unknown	1		7	7
		2		3	3
		3		5	5
					15
B	Yes Dependents	1	45	49	94
		2	8	25	33
		3	11	44	55
					182
C	No	1	107	172	279
		2	18	91	109
		3	23	130	153
					541
D	Not Applicable	1	38	35	73
		2	1	29	30
		3	6	27	33
					136
	COLUMN TOTAL		257	617	874*

* Four cases whose classification was unknown.

TABLE XI

132

Table XI revealed that where defendants clearly indicate dependents for whom they were responsible, 118 were held for bail while 64 were released, regardless of crime category in Group B. This group contained only 182 respondents, and their chance of release on recognizance because of dependents for whom they were responsible was one in three (64:182). Significantly, in Group B it was those in Crime Category One, which contains more offenses involving violence, who had a 50% chance of being released on recognizance (45:94). The highest number of cases fell in Crime Category One, regardless of dependent relationship.

In Group C, those who had no dependents, while nubering 541 cases in this sample, had a less than one in three chance to obtain release on recognizance (148:541). This seemed to indicate that: (1) while it was difficult to obtain ROR under any circumstances, the absence of responsibility for dependents weighs more heavily than responsibility for dependents; (2) in the only incidence where a dependency relationship was not applicable, e.g., a single man, more were released than held (38:35). This would indicate that a defendant's responsibility to others as a "social circumstance" of his possible pretrial parole was not considered favorably, nor was it considered consistently.

Analysis of Combined "Social Circumstances" And Forms of Release

This section tested the determination of pretrial release on recognizance against the combined social circumstances of age, marital status and dependents to discover if the relationship of the combined factors offers a picture of the release on recognizance different from what the preceding tables have shown in an examination of age, marital status and dependents in a singular fashion.

In Group A, defendants between 21 and 30 who were married with dependents, fewer than one in three (25:83) had a chance to be released on recognizance. In the same group, defendants without children had one chance in two (24:51) to be released. The critical factor, in deciding who is released on recognizance (which is a non-monetary form of release) cannot have been these social circumstances. It will have to be

AGE, MARITAL STATUS, AND DEPENDENTS
AS RELATED TO RELEASE ON RECOGNIZANCE

GROUP A

Age 21 - 30	ROR	Held For Bail	Row Total
Married W/Dependents	25	58	83
Married W/O Dependents	24	27	51
COLUMN TOTAL	49	85	134
			15.2% of all cases

GROUP B

Age 21 - 30	ROR	Held For Bail	Row Total
Single W/Dependents	1	6	7
Single W/O Dependents	106	256	362
COLUMN TOTAL	107	262	369
			42% of all cases

TABLE XII

found among the following factors: residence, employment, or the nature of the offense. It is important to
establish that a major aspect of the criteria of bailability has not been weighed carefully for all men in
Group A, for it would be reasonable to assume that those
with dependents would have greater argument for release
than those without. Evidently this is not the case.

Group B illustrates the phenomenon of single
men between 21 and 30 with dependents. This group,
while unusual, would illustrate a need for release as
they are the sole support of these dependents. In only
one case out of seven was a man in this category
released on recognizance. It becomes quite clear that
other factors than "social circumstances" of the defendant receive greater weight in the determination
of pretrial release on recognizance.

Out of 19 men who were between 21 and 30 who had
common-law marriages, none were "ROR'd" regardless of
dependents. This indicates an attitude toward common-
law marriage significantly different from that of
licensed marriage. Also out of seven men who were
divorced, five were "ROR'd" regardless of children.
There were no widowers in the 21-30 age sample. The
disparity of treatment between men in common-law
marriages and divorced men, whether dependents were in
the relationship or not, and regardless of crime
category, indicates the presence of a judgment, con-
scious or unconscious, extraneous to the release
decision: divorce is legal and common-law marriage
is beyond the law. Those who practice common-law
marriage are therefore a poorer risk for release.

Among all cases 57.2% are in the 21-30 age
bracket. The other significant numerical grouping is
those between 31 and 40. In Table XIII it will be seen
if the 31-to-40 age group who are in some marriage
relationship with dependents are treated any differently than the younger men.

Group C will look at divorced men, Group E will
examine the common-law relationship, and Group E those
whose marital status is unknown. This last group
consists of men who were reluctant to divulge personal
information.

AGE, MARITAL STATUS AND DEPENDENTS
AS RELATED TO RELEASE ON RECOGNIZANCE AND BAIL

GROUP C

Age 31 - 40	ROR	Held For Bail	Row Total
Divorced With Dependents	17	30	47
Divorced Without Dependents	13	19	32
COLUMN TOTAL	30	49	79

GROUP D

	ROR	Held For Bail	Row Total
Common Law With Dependents	0	0	0
Common Law Without Dependents	7	37	44
COLUMN TOTAL	7	37	44

GROUP E

	ROR	Held For Bail	Row Total
Unknown Marital Status With Dependents	1	3	4
Unknown Marital Status Without Dependents	18	95	113
COLUMN TOTAL	19	98	117

TABLE XIII

In Group C, divorced men continued to fare better than men in Group D, common-law marriages. Divorced men without dependents had just less than one in two chances of being ROR'd (13:32), while men in common-law marriage with dependents had less than one chance in six of being ROR'd (7:44).

Group E contained men of "unknown marital status." This group includes those who refused to indicate their family relationships. It was significant to note the size of this group and how their reluctance to admit their relationships and thus possibly involve the "family" militated against their pretrial parole. In the 31-40 age group there was only one single person. There were eight widowers, only one of whom was ROR'd, and seven divorced men, only two of whom were ROR'd.

These figures indicated that the combined factors of age, marital status and dependents play no positive role in the determination of "social circumstances" as required by the Code of Criminal Procedure. The evidence indicates that men were more likely to be held than released, regardless of these social circumstances.

In the 41 to 50 age group the following figures emerged: Out of five single men, only one was ROR'd. There was only one divorced man and one common-law marriage, and they were not ROR'd.

In the 51-60 age group, out of nine single men, seven were ROR'd. There was one widower not ROR'd, and of seven divorced men, three were ROR'd. These were the only entries. In the over-61 age bracket, the married man was released and the single man held. In these latter cases there are too few instances to draw firm conclusions.

Release on Recognizance and Residence

The remaining social factor examined in relation to ROR is residence. Table XIV delineates this relationship. Out of eight hundred and seventy-eight (878) cases, seven hundred and sixty-four (764) were residents and one hundred and fourteen (114) were non-residents of New York City. There were two hundred and fifty-seven (257) cases of ROR with two hundred and thirty-four (234) residents, and twenty-three (23) non-residents.

LENGTH OF RESIDENCE IN NEW YORK CITY
RELATIVE TO RELEASE ON RECOGNIZANCE

Residence	R O R Bail Under $100	$251-500	$501-1000	Total
Non-Resident	23			23
Less than 1 year	9			9
1 - 2 years	9			9
3 - 5 years	30	1		31
Over 5 years	184		1	185
TOTAL	255	1	1	257

TABLE XIV

Table XIV shows that the highest incidence of cases was among those who have had residence in New York City over five years and had an initial bail determination of less than $100.00. This would indicate that there was a direct correlation between the variable of ROR and length of residence, given this high number of instances. These figures also showed that the largest number of arraignments were for long-term residents. In the ensuing section on bail bond it will be seen that the number of instances of arraignments in the over-five-year resident category dominated the table also. See Tables XX-XXI. The following were evident from the relationship of ROR to residence. First, only two people with initial bail over $100 were released on recognizance out of two hundred and fifty-seven (257). Second, non-residents had a chance for ROR slightly better than one in four (223:114). Residents had a slightly less than one in three chance for ROR (234:764) regardless of length of residence. Third, what was most significant was that the highest number of RORs (185) were in the over-five-year resident category. This indicated less the optimum chance for release than the high number of arraignments among long-term residents. Fourth, the

evidence that ROR occurred among those whose initial
bail is $100 or less indicated that their possibility
of release bore directly on the nature of the offense
for which they are arraigned, rather than any other
factor. For example, no one with bail over $1,000 was
considered eligible for ROR, and only two, as noted,
were allowed ROR whose initial bail was between $250
and $1,000.

Summary of Analysis of ROR Cases

There were one hundred and sixty-four (164) RORs
in the age category 21-30, regardless of nature of
offense (see Table V). The greatest frequency of RORs
(190) occurred in crime category one, which includes
the most serious crimes (see Table VI and Footnote 6).
The largest number of RORs occurred among single men
(144) regardless of crime category (Table IX). Table
Ic showed that 148 men, clearly without dependents,
and regardless of crime category, had more RORs than
any other category, including those with dependents
(Ib). Finally, 185 of 257 RORs according to Table XIV,
were for men who had lived in New York City over five
years.

The following profile emerges from this accumulated data: Single men between the ages of 21 and 30
had a higher incidence of ROR than all other men. Men
who have lived in New York City more than five years
had a higher incidence of ROR than any other group.
Men with no dependents were ROR'd more than any other
group. Men with offenses in crime category one were
ROR'd more than any other group. There were also
likely to have had initial bail set under $100.

This suggests that there was no consistent,
direct correlation among any of the social factors
that have been analyzed and ROR. For example, married
men with dependents are less likely to be released on
recognizance than others. Traditional assumptions in
the use of ROR have been that it was for men who have
dependents or family responsibilities which were
indicative of stability in the community and whose loss
to that family might have been an unnecessary hardship.
The evidence did not support this argument. What did
appear was that young single men, most of whom have
lived in New York over five years and who have no
dependent or family responsibility, were released
regardless of the crime category. There is no evidence to indicate that these single men were more or

less stable than married men.

The purpose of ROR has been to provide a mechanism of non-monetary release based on criteria of community stability which will assure the reappearance in court of those released when required by the court. What emerged was that these social factors were inconsistently applied and that more single men were arraigned and released than any other group. The relationship between social circumstances of the defendant and release on recognizance was dysfunctional.

The Relation of Cash and Bail Bonds to the Social Circumstances of the Defendants

Traditionally it has been stated that there is a direct correlation between the dollar amount of bail and the nature of the violation of the penal law.[9] The variable "nature of the offense" should bear a direct correlation with the amount of bail along with the other required variables. The social circumstances of the defendant will be assessed in relation to dollar bail.

Bail and Crime Category

Table XV examines the relationship of the amount of bail from one dollar through those over five thousand dollars in relation to Sections 100.00 to 150.05 of the Penal Law with age as the dependent variable and crime category as the independent variable. This section of the penal law included index crimes such as murder, arson, assault, sexual offenses and burglary.

The table shows that more than half of all the cases in this study fall into this Penal Law grouping (456/878). The highest incidence of alleged violations were among the youngest group, 21 to 30, with 282 instances regardless of bail amount. Regardless of the age grouping, the greatest frequency of dollar bail was in the $1 to $99 range with 195 instances. This disclosed while this range of Penal Law violations contained many serious crimes they were frequently reduced from felony to misdemeanor status to be prosecuted in criminal court. This was sustained by the direct relationship between nature of offense and bail amount. As noted earlier, only one in fourteen cases went to Supreme Court. The

DISTRIBUTION OF BAIL AMOUNTS+
IN RELATION TO CRIME CATEGORY

Criminal Law Section 100.00-150.05 Age of Def.	1-99	100-250	251-500	501-1000	1001-2500	2501-5000	Other*	Row Total
21-30	125	2	64	44	29	15	3	782
31-40	40	4	35	15	14	8		116
41-50	17		9	4	6			36
51-60	9		2	1	1	2		15
61-	4		1	1	1			7
Column Total	195	6	111	65	51	25	3	456 / 878 or 51.9%

+ See Table XXIII For Bail Reductions
* Includes Unknowns

TABLE XV

141

evidence that bail was set under $100 in 195 cases showed that the court desired to place constraint on the defendant even if it is minimal. The kind of constraint chosen was financial. Tables XXIII and XXIV will show the ability of defendants to post bail to satisfy this constraint.

There was a consistent pattern of relationship between bail amount and crime category one (Sections 100.00 to 150.05 of the Penal Law). Two hundred and eighty-two (282) men between the ages of 21 and 30 have bail set between $1 and $5,000 with three cases beyond that figure or of unknown amount. One hundred twenty-five (125) of two hundred eighty-two (282) have bail less than $100. The remainder are in an inverse relation to the amount of bail; that is, as the amount of bail increases, the number of cases declines.

The same was true for age. The number of cases declined as the age of the defendant increases. This did not reveal either a leniency towards the younger, who have bail set over $250 in 155 cases, nor to the over-30 age group whose bail amounts distribute similarly to those under 30. It indicated rather that the court tried to reduce the charge to close the case but it was able to do this in just less than half the cases. It indicated that in this sample the older one got the less likely he was to be involved in a criminal arraignment proceeding. The only significant difference was the existence of only six (6) cases in the range of $100 to $250. This indicated that bail is generally set in multiples of $50. Thus, in the $1 to $99 range, most bails are $50 while in the $251 to $500 range most bails are also reduced to $50; that is, in the latter example, the judge would give the option of $500 bond or $50 cash bail (10%). The "multiple of fifty" rule did not work in the $100 to $250 range.

Table XVI relates the bail amount to age with crime category held constant. In this table the second generalized crime category covered sections 150.10 to 200.05 of the Penal Law. These sections included larceny, robbery and bribery.

DISTRIBUTION OF BAIL AMOUNTS
IN RELATION TO CRIME CATEGORY

Criminal Law Section 150.10-200.05 Age of Def.	1-99	100-250	251-500	501-1000	1001-2500	2501-5000	Other	Row Total
21-30	18	1	54	27	25	7	4	106
31-40	5		13	9	14	4	1	46
41-50	2	1	7	2	4	2	1	19
51-over	2					2		4
Column Total	27	2	44	38	43	15	6	175
								878

TABLE XVI

In the above table there was a marked contrast to Table XV as there are more incidents of bail over $250 than below it. However, the range $100 to $250 still has no statistical significance. The highest number of alleged violations occurs in the 21 to 30 age group (106). However, unlike Table XV only eighteen (18) out of 106 were bailable at less than $100. This was one in six (1:6). The same pattern held for those over thirty which would indicate that the nature of the offense was more significant than the age of the defendant. The largest frequencies were in the $1 to $99 range (27) and the ranges from $251 to $2500, namely 44, 38 and 43 respectively. This conforms to the "multiple of fifty" rule. Table XVI resembled Table XV in that the number of cases declined overall as the age of the defendants increased.

Table XVII presented the same variable relationships with the criminal category covering Sections 200.10 to the end of the Penal Law. The actual criminal sections go up to 270.15 only. Then there was a gap to the 400s where administrative procedures begin. The violations between 200 and 270 covered drug related acts and offenses against public health, morals and safety. The principal areas of violations were narcotics and weapons. Here again are found the highest number of cases among the youngest group. These were principally crimes related to drugs and weapons violations.

Table XVIII showed the distribution of type of bail in relation to both age and crime category. ROR = 0.00 bail. Taking the three types of pretrial release and ranking them in order of number of cases, it will be observed that bail bond had the most cases (472), release on recognizance was second (257) and cash bail third (149). It was also observed that cash bail reflected an aspect of bail bond. That is, it was a mechanism to afford a form of pretrial release for those who were unable to purchase a bail bond and who were also deemed unqualified for release on recognizance. Cash bail was 10% of the face value of a bail bond. It was notable that out of six hundred twenty-one (621) bail cases, exclusive of ROR, only one hundred and forty-nine (149) were able to obtain a cash reduction. This phenomenon will be further examined in Tables XXIII and XXIV.

144

DISTRIBUTION OF BAIL AMOUNTS
IN RELATION TO CRIME CATEGORY

Criminal Law Section 200.10-300.00 Age of Def.	1-99	100-250	251-500	501-1000	1001-2500	2500-5000	Other	Row Total
21-30	27	4	64	18	31	7	4	155
31-49	7	2	23	9	11	8		60
41-50	3	11	6	4	3	2		29
51-60	5		3	1				9
61-						1		1
Column Total	42	17	96	32	45	18	4	254 878 254

29.1%
Total

TABLE XVII

AGE AND CRIME CATEGORY
CROSS TABULATED WITH BAIL
BY TYPE AND AMOUNT

Age	Cat.	Bail Bond	1-50	CASH 51-100	101-500	ROR	Total
21-30	1	114	13	23	11	121	282
	2	80	1	4	4	17	106
	3	87	13	16	6	26	148
31-40	1	58	5	7	7	39	116
	2	35	2		3	6	46
	3	37	5	8	3	7	60
41-50	1	14	1	4		17	36
	2	12	3		2	2	19
	3	23		2	1	3	29
51-60	1	5	1	2	1	9	18
	2	2				2	4
	3	5		1		4	10
Totals		472	44	67	38	257	878

TABLE XVIII

In the Table XVIII the following facts were
clear. First, the majority of offenders were in crime
category one, regardless of age. Crime category three
had the second highest number of instances. Second,
the majority of offenses were committed by those in the
21-30 age bracket. The number of cases declined in
direct relation to the advancing age of the defendants.
Third, fewer than one in three had bail bond reduced to
the 10% cash option. This option may not have been
effectuated because the defendants were financially
poor. This meant cash bail, their only hope of release, aside from ROR, when bail was set was effectively removed from their reach. This made pretrial
detention a practical certainty.

146

Marital Status and Bail

Table XIX examines the marital status of defendants relative to bail amount and crime category. Five categories of relationships were chosen to allow for as much differentiation in status as possible. These categories include: unknown--where the defendant refuses to divulge or may have a homosexual relationship; single; widowed; divorced; licensed marriage; and common-law marriage followed the traditional definitions.

BAIL RELATIVE TO MARITAL STATUS

Marital Status	Cri. Cat.	Bail Bond	1-50	51-100	101-500	ROR	Total
Unknown	1	13		1	2	3	19
	2	3	1				4
	3	11		1			12
Single	1	126	11	20	15	107	279
	2	86	3	4	6	15	114
	3	100	14	20	6	22	162
Widowed	1	1		1		1	3
	2						
	3	1					1
Divorced	1	4	1			6	11
	2	6				1	7
	3	2					2
Married	1	46	7	14	3	72	142
	2	33	2		3	10	48
	3	33	4	6	3	18	64
Common-Law	1	1				1	2
	2	1				1	2
	3	5	1				6
Totals		472	44	67	38	257	878

TABLE XIX

Table XIX showed that the highest number of
defendants were in the single and married status groups,
eight hundred and eight (808) cases. These cases appear
as follows, regardless of crime category. Of five
hundred and fifty-four (554) single defendants, three
hundred twelve (312) were required to post bond (56%);
ninety-nine (99) were able to post cash bail (17%), and
one hundred and forty-four (144) were ROR'd (26%).
There were two hundred fifty-four (254) married men,
one hundred twelve (112) were required to post bail
bond (44%); forty-two (42) were able to post cash bail
(16%); and one hundred (100) were ROR'd (39%). These
statistics show that married men had no better chance
for release on cash bail than single men. They had a
three-to-two ratio of ROR (39%:25%), which gave them
a slight advantage over single men. A slightly smaller
percent of married men had to obtain a bail bond when
compared to single men (44%:56%), giving them a small
consideration in pretrial release. It was clear that
single men were treated more harshly than married men
in terms of type of release, except for cash bail.
However, single men made up more than half the number
of defendants. It was then necessary to see what
factors accounted for the release of married men over
single men, when crime category was held constant.
Several reasons suggest themselves. First, the
presence of dependents; second, residence; third,
economic factors. The first two shall be examined
presently, the third will be developed in the next
chapter. One thing certain: the marital status of
the defendant makes no dramatic difference in prospects
for pretrial release.

Dependents' Relationship and Bail

Table XX will examine the opportunity for
release based on bail categories of bond or cash bail,
which is 10% of the face value of the bond and comparatively easier to obtain if the defendant had some
resources.

DEFENDANTS' DEPENDENTS AND BAIL FORM

Group	Dependents For Whom Responsible	Crime Category	Bail Bond	CASH 1-50	CASH 51-100	CASH 101-500	ROR	Row Total
A	Unknown	1	6			1		7
		2	3					3
		3	5					5
B	Yes	1	35	4	9	2	45	95
		2	23			2	8	33
		3	32	2	7	3	11	55
C	None	1	126	12	21	14*	107	281
		2	80	4	4	3	18	109
		3	92	15	18	6	23	154
D	Not Applicable	1	24	3	6	2	38	73
		2	23	2		4	1	30
		3	23	2	2		6	33
COLUMN TOTAL			472	44	67	38	257	878

* Contains one cash bail case over $500.

TABLE XX

In Group A only one defendant (1:15) was able to post cash bail, all others had to post bond. In Group B, out of 119 cases who had dependents, excluding ROR, only 29 were able to secure cash bail release, or one in four. Among those in Crime Category 1, thirty-five (35) had to post bond; fifteen (15) were unable to secure release on cash bail. In Crime Category 2, twenty-three (23) had to post bond and two (2) secured release on cash bail of between $101 and $500. In Crime Category 3, thirty-two (32) had to post bond, and twelve (12) were able to secure cash bail release. These figures showed that the responsibility for dependents was not the circumstance considered in the bail determination.

In Group C, those who had no responsibility for dependents, out of three hundred and ninety-three (393) cases of bail, excluding ROR, only ninety-eight (98) defendants were able to secure cash bail, or one in four. In Crime Category 1, thirty-seven (37) out of one hundred sixty-three (163), or one in four, were able to secure cash bail as a form of release. In Crime Category 2, eleven (11) out of ninety-one (91) were released on cash bail, and in Crime Category 3 thirty-nine (39) out of one hundred thirty-one (131), or just over one in three, were released. In Group D, out of ninety-one (91) cases, only twenty-one (21) were able to secure cash bail release, eleven (11) of those (49%) were in Crime Category 1. The conclusions which may be derived from this data show that one in four (149:617) were able to secure cash bail release regardless of dependents. That while there are more men held for bail without dependents in Groups C and D, their ratio of release was no better than for men with responsibility for dependents.

Residence and Bail

Table XXI delineated the relationship between length of residence and amount of bail, exclusive of ROR. The figures up to $250 were all cash bail, and those between $251 and $1,000 include cash and bail bond figures by subsection. There were no cash bail releases over $1,000. Of those sixteen (16) cash bail releases in the $500 to $1,000 range, fifteen (15) were for $500 and one was $1,000. All those over $1,000 were bail bonds.

150

RESIDENCE AND BAIL

CASH OR BAIL BOND

RESIDENCE	1-50	51-100	101-250	251-500 CB	251-500 BB	501-1000 CB	501-1000 BB	1001-2500	2501-5000	Other	Total
Non-Resident		1		12	23	2	24	18	10	1	91
Less Than 1 Yr.		1	5	4	4	2	7	7	2	3	34
1 - 2 Yr.		1	1	3	3	2	2	5	1		18
3 - 5 Yr.	1			7	8		5	10	3	1	35
Over 5 Yr.	1	4	8	92	99	11	83	101	38	6	443
COLUMN TOTAL	2	7	14	118	136	16	121	141	54	11	621

TABLE XXI

151

RESIDENCE AND RELEASE RATIO

TYPE OF RELEASE

RESIDENCE	ROR Cases	Bail Cases	Ratio
Non-Resident	23	91	1:4
Less Than 1 Yr.	9	34	1:4
1 - 2 Yr.	9	18	1:2
3 - 5 Yr.	31	35	1:1.1
Over 5 Yr.	185	443	1:2.4
	257	621	

TABLE XXII

The two important facts to emerge from Table XXI were as follows. First, four hundred forty-three (443) out of six hundred twenty-one (621) defendants, or 71%, resided in New York City more than five years. This fact combined with earlier data on defendants' ages would strongly indicate these defendants had long residence in New York. Second, the majority of bailments, whether cash or bond, fell in the range from $251 to $2,500, regardless of length of residence. This indicates that length of residence plays no significant part in the determination of pretrial release. Table XXII sets the ratio of ROR to all other bail forms. It appeared that longer residents have a slight advantage over non-residents and short-term residence factor or volume of cases cannot be established. What was clear was that length of residence played no important part in determining pretrial release.

MAJOR BAIL CATEGORIES*

BAIL POSTED

	1-99	100-250	251-500	501-1000	1001-2500	2501-5000	Over 5000	Total
Yes	3	3	17	8	3	1	1	36
No	4	9	116	110	127	51	10	427

POSTED AT ARRAIGNMENT

	1-99	100-250	251-500	501-1000	1001-2500	2501-5000	Over 5000	Total
At Arrignment	3	3	10	3	1			20
Later			7	5	2	1	1	16
Original	3	3	15	4	2		1	28
Reduced			2	4	1	1		8

* Based on frequency of cases. Cash and Bond (six cases unaccounted)

TABLE XXIII

153

Was Bail Posted?

The central question, having examined these social factors, was to determine for these 621 cases if bail was posted, was it the original or reduced amount, and how much. Table XXIII indicates the major "bail categories," that is, those with the highest number of instances. Table XXIV treats the minor "bail categories" or those with fewer instances.

Table XXIII delineated clearly that in "major" categories, those with the highest number of instances, only thirty-six (36) out of a total of four hundred sixty-three (463) defendants were able to post bail in any form. Of the thirty-six (36), twenty (20) were able to post bail at arraignment and sixteen (16) had to spend some time in detention before pretrial release. Of the same thirty-six (36), twenty-eight (28) posted the original amount and eight (8) were allowed to post a reduced amount. The importance of this data cannot be overlooked. That while bail was always set, in no case were a majority of defendants able to post bail regardless of amount, and that only 8% of those in these major categories were able to secure release at all. Table XXIV demonstrates the same pattern.

MINOR BAIL CATEGORIES*
WAS BAIL POSTED

	1 99	100 250	251 500	500 1000	1001 2500	2501 5000	Total
Yes		1	37	5	2	1	46
No	6	1	81	11	4	1	106
At Arraignment			24	3			27
Later		1	13	2	2	1	19
Original		1	29	3			33
Reduced			8	2	2	1	13

* Based on frequency of bail cases, cash or bond, relative to age and offense.

TABLE XXIV

154

SUMMARY AND CONCLUSIONS

The evidence presented in the sections above indicated there was no direct correlation among these social circumstances of the defendant -- age, marital status, dependents, and residence -- and his ability to obtain release before trial in any of the three forms. This lack of correlation raised serious questions about the application of all of the criteria of bailability in the determination of release. The evidence supported the judgment of the Vera Institute of Justice in its report on Overcrowding in the Detention Institutions of New York City,[10] that while there were criteria of bailability, there were no rules governing their application.

The data showed that of 878 clients of the Legal Aid Society in 1970-71, only 38.6% were able to secure any form of pretrial release. Of this group, 257 were those released on recognizance. The remainder, as shown in Tables XXIII and XXIV, had to spend some time in detention or were released on bail when funds could be raised for their release, or bail was reduced. The only cases of release at arraignment which were clearly unimpeded by money were those 257 released on recognizance. What was most important in the analysis of the ROR cases was that there was no precise differentiation of criteria of release among the bail forms relative to social circumstances, as in Table IV, where with age and crime category held constant, more defendants were held for bond than ROR'd. Table V showed that younger men compose 85.3% of all defendants, yet there was no difference in their treatment from older men.

Married men in Crime Category 1, according to Table VIII, had an equal chance for ROR or bail, but this did not apply to married men in any other crime category. This indicated that it was the nature of the offense which was a stronger determining factor in the type of release offered. Single men, as Table VIII showed, had consistently poorer chances for ROR than any other group. This suggested the negative correlation based on status but it has to be relevant to other related factors. These factors will be seen in Chapter V. Table X showed that having dependents for whom the defendant was responsible provided no positive correlation in obtaining release. Consistently, more men with dependents were held than were released. Tables XII and XIII show the combined social factors of age, marital status and dependents relative

155

to release. One would expect that married men with
families, younger or older, would have some stronger
grounds for pretrial release than single men without
dependents. This clearly was not so. Finally, in
length of residence, as Table XIV showed, there was
some relationship of ROR. It was not ascertained that
the relationship of ROR to residence was based on
community stability. It did show that the largest
number of defendants were long term residents and a
greater proportion of them were likely to obtain ROR
than any other group. Considering the bail types of
bond and cash as differentiated from ROR, it was seen
that regardless of age, according to Table XV, defendants were most frequently in the bail ranges $1.00
to $99.00, and $251 to $1,000. The pattern was consis-
tent. This indicated that the bail determination had
no correlation with age. It does indicate that the
dollar determination had a consistent relation to the
nature of the offense, as the bail amounts remained
constant over the entire range of the penal code.

Table XIX showed that very few bail bonds were
actually reduced to the cash option, or in very few
cases was the cash option the first offer. Regardless
of marital status, bail was required with few conver-
sions to cash option or release on recognizance. This
indicated that the pretrial release system was closely
geared to ability to post a monetary form of release.
This suggested an imbalance between social and economic
circumstances of release which are to be evaluated
equally in the release criteria. Table XX shows for
bond what ROR shows, that dependents carry no positive
correlation in obtaining release. Tables XXI and XXII
pointed out that stable residence pattern did not
afford any better chance of release for those who had
monetary bond set than those ROR'd. A level of three-
to five-year residence, and above, only indicated a
greater number of cases and a slightly better chance
for ROR.

Finally, Tables XXIII and XXIV showed that
regardless of both type of monetary release and amount,
in no case were defendants more able to post the amount
required than not. Almost half had to spend some time
in detention until funds were raised. Fewer than one-
third had bail reduced to make posting more likely.
These facts indicated a rigidity in the bail system
that neglected the social circumstances of the defendants, who by constitutional right were innocent until
proven guilty. The stringency of the bail determination suggested that it was not safe to release a

156

defendant prior to trial because he was guilty.
This presumption of guilt was the result of the lack
of understanding and application of the social circumstances in the determination of suitability for pretrial
release.

FOOTNOTES

1. P. Lazarsfield. "Interpretation of Statistical Relations as a Research Operation," in Lazarsfield and Rosenberg, ed., The Language of Social Research. Illinois: Glencoe Free Press, 1955, pp. 115-125.

2. Code of Criminal Procedure, Sections 550-556. 1967 ed.

3. The 1972 Criminal Justice Plan. Executive Committee Criminal Justice Coordinating Council, p. 73.

4. See Code of Criminal Procedure, Section 550, case note 4, and Section 510.30 of The Criminal Procedure Law. New York: Gould Publications, 1972, pp. 193-194.

5. These factors appear on the "yellow sheet."

6. J. Locke, R. Penn, J. Rick, E. Bunten and G. Hare. Compilation and Use of Criminal Court Data in Relation to Pre-Trial Release of Defendants: Pilot Study. Washington, D.C.: National Bureau of Standards, 1970.

7. The crime categories are based on those found in McKinney's Consolidated Laws of New York, Volume 39, Parts One and Two, Penal Law. The Penal Law covers offenses by section and subsection from 1.00 to 400. Because of the complexity of enumeration, for tabulation of the offenses have been reduced to the following three categories roughly approximating the seriousness of the offenses.

    Category 1 = 100.00 to 150.05

    Category 2 = 150.10 to 200.05

    Category 3 = 200.10 to 270.15

    Category 1 includes offenses such as assault, homicide, conspiracy, sexual crimes, solicitation, burglary and arson. Category 2 includes larceny, robbery and bribery. Category 3 includes drug offenses and those against public health, safety and morals as well as weapons violations. The numbers from 270.15 to 400 are open for inclusion in the future of other offenses. The 400. numbers start administrative regulations.

8. See footnote 7, _supra_.

9. See Michael Pearl,"Hard Times on Bail Bond Row,"
   op. cit., p. 42, Freed and Wald, Bail and Summons:
   1965, Rankin op. cit., and footnote 6 supra.

10. See footnote 9, Chapter II.

CHAPTER V

THE ECONOMIC FACTORS IN THE
DETERMINATION OF BAIL

Introduction

The chief economic factors to be observed in the determination of bail for any defendant were: first, employment; second, ready cash; third, access to collateral. If the defendant had any of these three factors operating, the likelihood of obtaining release on bail was greater. If these factors did not pertain, then a period of detention was likely. This chapter will examine the relationship of bail to employment. It will look at the other sources of income for defendants and their bail type. Finally it will relate the type of bail to the case disposition of these defendants.

Employment at Arrest and Bail

The significance of gainful employment in the eyes of the court can be seen from the type of release offered and the employment of the defendant. Out of 878 cases in this study, 414 (47.1%) did not have a job when arrested, while 361 (41.1%) did, and for 103 (11.8%) this was not ascertained. Of the 361 employed men, 257 were released on recognizance. This was the only consistent pattern of release in the entire study. As Chapter IV showed, there was only negative correlation between social circumstances and pretrial release. The marital status, dependents and age, for example, do not weigh significantly in release. This clear economic correlation which was only a partial requirement of the law shows an ambivalence in the ajudication of bail at arraignment which amounts to an unconstitutional discrimination against those unemployed or with small financial resources. What became clear as one deals with these 878 cases in the criminal court was that life for them contains a great number of frustrations and complications from employment, education, housing, family life and self-image. As life got increasingly complex and the successful resolution of grievances and frustrations became harder, the combination of complexity and frustration led many defendants to chose to solve their problems in ways which were in violation of the law. It was significant to note that 80% of the cases in the study were members of minority groups - black American, Hispano-American and non-English-speaking immigrants from southern Europe.

Employment among these groups is often marginal. It is at or below the minimum wage, offers little security, and employment is sometimes seasonal. This leads to the kind of behavior which Merton calls "non-conforming rather than conforming conduct."[1] This results from the emphasis which our society places on economic affluence and social ascent for all its members regardless of social class. While non-conforming conduct is not due solely to economics, as Merton carefully notes,[2] a comparatively rigidified class structure with attendant problems of mobility may shut off a significant number of approved avenues of success with the result that unlawful routes to apparent economic success are sought.

The majority of the crimes in this study involved theft, larceny, drugs, and assault, as noted in Chapter IV, Table XV. This conforms to the premise of direct action to solve problems or satisfy needs. In the tables which follow, the income levels of these defendants reveal their economic status and attendant social circumstances. It becomes clear that by ordering bail in monetary terms the pattern of economic frustration continues.

E M P L O Y E D   A T   A R R E S T

AMOUNT OF BAIL

BAIL TYPE	$99	250	500	1000	2500	5000-over	TOTAL
ROR*	255		1		1		257
CASH	13	50	33				96
BOND	7	1					8
	275	51	34		1		361
							878
							41.1%/100%

*ROR = Zero dollars, but a dollar
       bail is asked and ROR is
       subsequently applied for.

TABLE I

162

Table I shows that employemnt counts heavily in
the defendant's pretrial release. This conforms to the
"Ideal Bail Risk Profile" as shown in Table II on page
62. All those released on recognizance were employed.
Keeping in mind that the cash bail option is not a
guarantee of release as Tables XXIII and XXIV in the
previous chapter showed, only 43 of 96 employed offered
cash release could utilize this option. This suggests
that the level of income even for the employed is quite
low.

UNEMPLOYED AT ARREST

AMOUNT OF BAIL

BAIL TYPE	$99	250	500	1000	2500	5000	5000+	Total
CASH		53						53
BOND		8	136	60	97	46	14	361
TOTAL*		61	136	60	97	46	14	414/878

47.1%/100%

* There are 103 cases (11.8%) whose
  employment circumstances do not
  appear because they were unclear.

TABLE II

Table II indicated a direct correlation between
the amount and type of bail and the defendant's unemployment. There was no bail below $99 for the
unemployed. The bail range held consistently to the
$250-$2500 range as it did in Tables XXIII and XXIV
in Chapter IV. There were only 53 offers of reduction
from bond to cash because defendants were clearly
without means. This showed that the court was willing
to be lenient with a defendant who had some means, but
chose no other option but to detain those who were
without means. Comparisons of Table I and Table II
revealed the pattern that those who were employed were
released without having to post any money or very
little money, while they might well afford some monetary

163

form of release. However, those unemployed could not
obtain this non-monetary form of release nor find a
dollar amount commensurate with their financial ability.

Table III shows that those who are not employed
were more likely to be detained than those employed,
and the unemployed had a slightly higher chance of
conviction and longer sentence if convicted.

EMPLOYMENT AND POST ARREST
STATUS   OUTCOME

DEFENDANT	EMPLOYED	UNEMPLOYED
Cleared	125	113
Guilty, No Prison	90	88
Guilty, Short Term	110	151
Guilty, Long Term	36	62
	361	414

TABLE III

Table III showed the shift of favorable outcome
from the first two entries for the employed; 125 were
cleared as opposed to 113 unemployed. Ninety employed
while judged guilty have prison terms suspended, to the
unfavorable outcome for the unemployed. Forty-one more
unemployed men spent time in prison than employed men
on short sentences. Twenty-six more unemployed men
spent long terms in prison than employed men. These
results reveal financial circumstances' impact upon
bail setting that was not just on pretrial circumstances
but on the final condition of the defendants. The
significance of Table III should lead to the questions:
first, why do a significant number of defendants get
cleared of the charges regardless of employment?
Second, why do a significant number get short-term
sentences? Table IV shows the outcome by pretrial
status by employment at arrest.

164

OUTCOME BY PRETRIAL STATUS BY EMPLOYMENT AT ARREST

OUTCOME DEFENDANT	EMPLOYED		UNEMPLOYED	
	Detained	Released	Detained	Released
Cleared	32	98	43	100
Guilty-no prison	41	48	36	77
Guilty-short term	78	31	90	20
Guilty-long term	32	1	43	5
TOTAL	183	178	212	202

TABLE IV

The key factor in obtaining clearance of charges and avoiding prison was correlated to ability to obtain pretrial release, as Table IV shows. Of the employed men, 98 out of 178 released men were cleared while only 32 of 183 detained men were cleared. The figures are consistent for the unemployed - 100 out of 202 released men are cleared while only 43 of 212 detained men are cleared. This establishes that it is less the fact of employment then detention itself which works against defendants.

The Relationship of Income and Bail

In order to understand the defendants' ability to obtain release a look at income was essential. Table V sets the average weekly income of defendants from any source.

AVERAGE WEEKLY INCOME

TYPE OF BAIL	$1 25	26 50	51 75	76 100	101 125	126 150	151 200	Other	Total
ROR	118	6	17	43	0	56	11	6	257
BOND	336	9	25	55	0	39	6	2	472
CASH	101	4	5	17	0	19	3	0	149
TOTAL	555	19	47	115	0	114	20	8	878

TABLE V

Of 878 cases, 736 had incomes less than one
hundred dollars per week from any source. These sources
included: earned income alone, 545; welfare supplement,
173; unemployment insurance, 13; support from another
family member, 108; and other sources, 39. These
figures showed that the majority of defendants were
from the wage-earner population with incomes below
one hundred dollars per week. A large number had incomes less than one hundred dollars a month. For these
there was some supplemental assistance but their
economic circumstances left no resources for monetary
bail. The resultant detention also led to the loss of
employment and the loss of welfare assistance.

The Relationship of Income, Bail and Outcome

Tables XXIII and XXIV in Chapter IV have shown
that there was a direct correlation between pretrial
status as released or detained, and the amount of bail
- the higher the amount, the smaller the number released. The outcome of the case was also related to
the amount of bail, as Table V has shown. Eighty-six
percent of those released on recognizance never got a
prison sentence, a rate twice as high as the group
having a bail amount set. Similarly, those released
on recognizance were far less likely to get long prison
sentences than those for whom bail was set at $1000 or
more.

OUTCOME BY BAIL AMOUNT

DEFENDANT	ROR	LESS THAN $500	$1000	OVER $1000	TOTAL
Cleared	96	62	30	32	220
Guilty-no prison	55	44	20	50	169
Guilty-short term	21	122	52	36	231
Guilty-long term	3	13	20	80	116
	175	241	122	198	736

TABLE VI

It can be shown that the amount of bail explained the disparity of outcome between detained and
released populations. It can be argued that the court
set bail in a manner which it presumed will correspond
to the final outcome of the case. The amount of bail
was thus a rough initial guess as to the likelihood
of conviction and/or length of sentence, if any.[3] If
this were so, those with like bail amounts should not
experience any gross difference in outcome whether they
raise bail or not.

Table VII related outcome by pretrial status
and bail amount.

Of those with bail less than $500, fewer than
one-third were released or "out" prior to trial (54/
187). Twenty-three percent of those detained or "in"
were cleared, while 37% of those out were cleared of
charges pending. This finding was significant in
showing that the outcomes were different even though
bail amounts were comparable. The same was true for
those with comparable bail over $1000. Two hundred
ninety-nine cases were held in detention, and 21 were
allowed out on pretrial parole. Of those detained,
only 19%, or 59 out of 299, were cleared, and of those
out on pretrial parole 33%, or 7 of 21, were cleared.

OUTCOME BY PRETRIAL STATUS AND BAIL AMOUNT

OUTCOME	LESS THAN $500		MORE THAN $1000	
DEFENDANT	IN	OUT*	IN	OUT
Cleared	43	20	59	7
Guilty-no prison	20	13	63	7
Guilty-short term	110	11	90	4
Guilty-long term	14	0	87	3
	187	54	299	21

* Excludes ROR

TABLE VII

The discrepancy in treatment between those detained and those released persisted even among cases which, by this reasoning, were viewed as comparable by the court which set bail. Two-thirds of those who made bail over $1000 will not serve a prison term even if convicted. Of those who cannot make $500 or less as bail, two-thirds will serve a prison term if convicted.

None of the factors explained the disparity between treatment and outcome of detained and released persons. It was unlikely that these factors in combination will, and in fact they do not, as Table XII in Chapter IV, has shown. When the factors of crime charged, prior record, marital status, dependents and employment were the same, defendants who were detained were 43% more likely to be convicted and sentenced to prison than those released pending trial. Pretrial status turned out to be more important than either the crime charged or prior record. Thus, the inability to post bail or obtain release on recognizance presented a significant likelihood of conviction and prison term for the defendant even when the case was comparable to a paroled defendant.

FOOTNOTES

1. Robert Merton, Social Theory and Social Structure. New York: The Macmillan Company, 1957, Chapter I.

2. Ibid., p. 118.

3. Legal Aid Study, p. 27.

4. Tables III, IV, VI and VII courtesy of the Legal Aid Society. See Legal Aid Study, p. 27f.

CHAPTER VI

RECORDS, CIRCUMSTANCES AND BAIL TYPE

Introduction

Having examined in detail the social and economic circumstances of these 878 defendants as they relate to bail, it must be determined what correlation, if any, exists between: first, the prior record of the defendant and the type of bail, and second, aggravated circumstances and bail. Aggravated circumstances would include being armed with a weapon, using it, causing injury and resisting arrest. It would seem that cases similar in every respect but these circumstances might have bail set differently. A distinction among variables of prior record (number of arrests and probation report) and nature of the offense (felony, violation, misdemeanor) by the judge would indicate a positive correlation in applying these criteria of bailability. It would remain to ask whether the same flexibility can be applied to those social circumstances which have, as this study shows, only a negative correlation.

Prior Arrest Record of Convictions and Type of Bail

The Code of Criminal Procedure[1] required that the magistrate consider the prior record of the defendant in the determination of bail. The Criminal Procedure Law of 1971 also requires the prior record's consideration but with an emphasis on court appearance if the defendant were released.[2] In the table which follows the general groupings of bail and prior record indicate the extent of their consideration. It is important to keep in mind that an arrest record was not the same as a conviction but the "Yellow Sheet" listed arrests but does not consistently record dispositions and convictions. It is possible for a man ajudged not guilty but with an arrest to experience treatment similar to a convicted man.

This table indicated that the largest aggregate of defendants (586) have more than one arrest. Slightly less than one-third (251/878) had no prior record of arrests or convictions. The record on 41 was not ascertained. However, each of these latter two groups of men, regardless of final disposition, will now have an arrest record.

PRIOR ARREST, CONVICTION RECORD AND TYPE OF BAIL

TYPE OF BAIL	PRIOR RECORD UNKNOWN	YES	NO	TOTAL
ROR	9	97	151	257
BOND	29	375	68	472
CASH	3	114	32	149
COLUMN TOTAL	41	586	251	878

TABLE I

Table I shows that 151 out of 251 men with no prior record received release on recognizance. The remaining 100 had a monetary choice. The monetary bail decision has to be based on factors other than record and socio-economic circumstances.

Three hundred seventy-five men with a record, out of 586, had to post a bond. In Chapter V, Tables II, III and IV showed the relation between the crime category and the amount of bond, the greatest number of bonds being between $250 and $1500. It was clear from Table I that the prior record of the defendant is significant in the determination of pretrial release, as 151 men with no record could be ROR'd while 375 men with a record had to post a bond.

Number of Prior Arrests and Bail

Table II related the number of prior arrests to the bail disposition. In tabulating the number of arrests there was no distinction made as to the nature of the arrest - felony, misdemeanor or violation - nor for evidence of conviction.

TABLE II

NUMBER OF ARRESTS	AMOUNT OF BAIL BOND							Row Total
	1-99	100-250	251-500	501-1000	1001-2500	2501-5000	Over 5000	
0	1	8	23	17	15	2	2	68
1-2	2	1	53	46	54	20	2	178
3-9	4	3	55	53	63	29	6	213
10 or more			5	5	1	1	1	13
Column Total	7	12	136	121	133	52	11	472

Table II established a direct correspondence between the amount of bail bond and the number of prior arrests. Only 3 men of 178 with one or two prior arrests had a bail bond $250 or less. Only 7 men of 213 with 3 to 9 arrests had bail set at $250 or less. It was also demonstrated that 32 of 68 (49%) bail bonds for those with no prior record of arrests were fixed in amounts of $500 or less. Only 56 of 178 (31%) of those with one or two arrests had bond fixed in amounts of $500 or less, while 62 of 213 (29%) of those with 3 to 9 arrests had bond fixed at $500 or less. The greatest number of bonds (390) fell in the $251 to $2500 range. This established a direct correlation between the number of prior arrests and bail amount. In Chapter V, Tables II, III and IV, it has been shown how the nature of the offense is also directly correlated with the amount of bail bond, sustaining the hypothesis that the two most significant factors in the bail determination were the nature of the offense and the prior record.

Table III showed that as the number of arrests increased, the likelihood of release on low bail decreased.

NUMBER OF ARRESTS	ROR $0	AMOUNT OF CASH BAIL				TOTAL
		1-50	51-100	101-500	Other	
0	151	9	14	9	-	183
1-2	70	21	30	15	-	136
3-9	34	11	2	15	-	82
10 or more	2	1	1	--	1	5
Column Subtotal		42	67	39	1	
COLUMN TOTAL	257			149		406

TABLE III

174

The chance of a defendant's having bail $50 or less with no arrests was 90%, or 160 out of 183. The chance of release for $50 or less with one or two arrests was 65% or 91 out of 136, and with three or more arrests 55%, or 48 out of 87. There can be no question of the significance of the number of prior arrests in the cash bail determination when the chances for such release decrease 35% once a defendant had at least three prior arrests. The importance of prior arrests in bail setting was that they were one of the few pieces of hard data available to the judge at the time these cases were arraigned. It was data immediately available and readily checked, unlike the social data the defendant must supply.

The Relationship of Office of Probation Recommendation and Bail

The problem of ascertaining the likelihood of a defendant's appearance in court when required was demonstrated in the following two tables. The data here were based on the official Office of Probation Reports.[3] The report's determination of likelihood of appearance was based on data such as employment, residence, family ties and references which constituted social circumstances. The availability of this specific evidence determined the positive recommendation for release. What became clear from studying these reports was that they are frequently incomplete and that they were unable to provide the needed information.

Table IV showed that the Office of Probation was only able to offer a positive recommendation for 41 out of 472 (8%) of bondable defendants. Probation did discover another charge pending in 92 of 472 cases (20%) which would make these defendants ineligible for pretrial parole. The largest figures were for unavailable references (32%) or 152 out of 472 cases. If the references had been available, would this have altered the judgment on likelihood of appearance? When problems of insufficient staff to gather data on defendants was added to other information problems - such as wrong phone numbers and addresses, misspellings, and similar inadequacies - (29 plus 106), 135 out of 472 cases are incomplete (29%). When this

RECOMMENDATION OF OFFICE OF PROBATION

DEFENDANT	AMOUNT OF BAIL BOND						
	1-99	100-250	251-500	501-1000	1001-2500	2501-over	ROW TOTAL
Likely to appear	3	1	16	11	9	1	41
+Wanted on other charge	1		24	23	27	17	92
References unavailable	2	5	50	33	40	22	152
Refused interview			4	4	3	2	13
*Another case pending			6	2	9	4	21
Excluded (homicide)							
Insufficient staff to check			6	13	7	3	29
Other information problems	1	4	27	29	34	11	106
Reason not ascertained		2	3	6	4	3	18
Column Total	7	12	136	121	133	63	471

+ Violation of parole, bail jumping, etc.

* Defendant on parole when arrested

TABLE IV

176

figure was considered with unavailable references, 152 out of 472 (32%), there are 287 cases or 61% of all Probation Recommendations which are incomplete. The lack of information, lack of time or staff to verify, plus inaccuracies in information militate against the defendants' chance to have a recommendation which would illuminate the contents of the "yellow sheet," or prior record.

It can only be surmised that any of the 61% of the insufficient reports would have altered the bail bond status of any defendant. However, such a large percentage of deficient reports confirmed the negative correlation which had been shown for social circumstances of defendants in Chapter IV, and the limitations of the criminal justice system's ability to insure a balanced presentation of the defendants' situations.

The same pattern held true for cash bail as Table V shows. Perhaps the only significant differences between Table IV and Table V were the high number of positive recommendations and the high number of unavailable references which, for some reason, did not militate against release on recognizance. This again confirms the evidence that the nature of the offense plays the most significant role in these ROR determinations.

Table V illustrated one major factor in bail determination. That pretrial parole was ultimately the prerogative of the judge. In the ROR determinations we know that all 257 defendants were released. Clearly, then, it was the prerogative of the judge to release despite an adverse recommendation, viz., wanted on another charge (6), refused interview (2), another case pending (8), exclude this case (2). It is the judge's prerogative to release when the report was incomplete, viz., references unavailable (85), insufficient staff to obtain data (11), information problems (39), and other reasons (8). In all ROR determinations in this sample the judges had 96 positive recommendations - 96 out of 257 or 36%, they had 18 negative recommendations - 143 out of 257 or 55%. On what grounds were these determinations made? The usual explanation is judicial "discretion." It has been pointed out in Chapter IV[4] that discretion can only take place in the presence of full information according to Wilkins[5] in order to be truly discretion and a rational act. What was seen here was judicial prerogative based on inadequate information, not

177

RECOMMENDATION OF OFFICE OF PROBATION	ROR	AMOUNT OF CASH BAIL				
DEFENDANT	$0	1-50	51-100	101-500	Other	Row Total
Likely to appear	96	6	4	4	--	110
+Wanted on other charge	6	6	2	6	--	20
References unavailable	85	18	28	11	--	142
*Another case pending	8	2	7	2	--	19
Exclude case	2				--	2
Insufficient staff	11	1	5	2	--	19
Other information problems	39	11	19	8	--	77
Reasons not ascertained	8		1		5	14
Column Total	257	44	67	33	5	406

TABLE V

discretion, which demonstrated that the administration of criminal justice in the Manhattan Criminal Court still was not as evaluative as criminal procedure required, and that justice at this level had a random quality to it.[6] This resulted from the practical impossibility of acquiring all the data stipulated under the Code of Criminal Procedure.[7] Thus genuine discretion became an impossibility.

The arbitrary nature of the determination of pretrial parole was clearly functional in these ROR cases. It was less clearly functional, but nonetheless present in the determination of: first, whether bail will be set at a predetermined amount for a specified charge independent of circumstances; second, whether that bail would be reduced in amount or in kind as Tables XXIII and XXIV show in Chapter IV.

What emerged from an examination of these bail types in relation to the recommendation of the Office of Probation was that sometimes they were applied to a defendant's advantage regardless of the negative or insufficient report in ROR cases, and sometimes they were applied to a defendant's disadvantage by a judge's insistence on bail bond or cash bail regardless of a favorable report on the defendant's likelihood of appearance. Table IV shows that 41 defendants had to post bond regardless of a favorable recommendation, and Table V shows that 14 had to post cash regardless of a positive recommendation.

In the cash bail category there were only 14 positive recommendations (9%). There were 26 negative recommendations (17%), and 109 incomplete recommendations (74%). A rate of incompleteness this high was indicative of inadequate performance of investigative duties. There can be no question that complete data in these 109 cash bail cases would possibly enable some of these defendants to find some other means to obtain release, either ROR or at a lesser cost. The Office of Probation indicates only that it had insufficient information to complete the reports or inadequate staff. The question must also be asked that Foote[8] and Goffman asked.[9] Do those in the criminal justice system judge the defendant as guilty before the fact? There can be no doubt from the evidence presented that a commitment to the premise "every man is innocent until proven guilty" was lacking in the gathering of this data. The proof of this was that the necessary data has been gathered in all 878 cases in this study with very minor exceptions as noted in each table.

Aggravated Circumstances and Type of Bail

In addition to the social, economic and procedural data factors which have been examined, there remained one basis on which the bail determination might conceivably be made. This area was called the weight of evidence factor in the bail procedure.[10] For our purposes it was called aggravated circumstances. This category included whether or not the defendant was armed with a weapon, whether it was used, what injury was sustained by the victim and was force used in resisting arrest. These variables will help determine if there was any significant difference in the bail cases with aggravated and those without aggravated circumstances.

One hundred sixty-two defendants were armed with a weapon in the offense for which they were arraigned.

ARMED WITH WEAPON AND BAIL BOND

	AMOUNT							
ARMED	1-99	100-250	251-500	501-1000	1001-2500	2501-5000	Over 5000	ROW TOTAL
YES	1	2	13	20	31	23	4	94
NO	6	10	122	100	101	29	7	375
UNKNOWN			1	1	1			3
COLUMN TOTAL	7	12	136	121	133	52	11	472

TABLE VI

Ninety-four of all bond cases involved the use of a weapon (25%). The greatest frequency distribution for armed with weapon was 31 in the bond range of \$1001 to \$2500. It is evident that being armed with a weapon warrants bail over \$500 in 78 out of 94 cases (83%). Where there was no weapon bail bond was set under \$500 in 138 of 375 such cases (37%), but under \$500 where weapons are involved in only 16 out of 94 cases (17%). It is shown that being armed with a weapon was an aggravated circumstance and carries significant weight in the bail determination.

Table VII showed that weapons were a factor in cash bail release and ROR.

It was significant that 39 defendants were ROR'd even though weapons were an issue in their cases; 29 had to post cash for a total of 68. The most common weapon in criminal acts was the knife. Clearly the type of pretrial release was reflective of an ability to distinguish, first, among weapons, and second the weapon's place in the crime.

ARMED WITH WEAPON AND CASH BAIL

ARMED WITH WEAPON	ROR $0	1-50	AMOUNT OF CASH BAIL 51-100	101-500	ROW TOTAL
YES	39	7	14	8	68
NO	216	38	52	28	334
UNKNOWN	2		1	1	4
COLUMN TOTAL	257	45	67	37	406

TABLE VII

In 159 cases the weapon was wielded by the defendant and in three cases by an accomplice. Further, the presence of a weapon led to injury in 92 of 162 cases (57%). No injury was reported in 70 cases (43%). In 27 of 92 cases (29%) where there were serious injuries, defendants were ROR'd. This would indicate that injury to the victim was not as significant in the determination of bail, as being armed with a weapon was, ironically.

Finally, resistance to arrest only occurred in 48 of 878 cases, or 5.4%, and was not statisitically significant in terms of the bail proceedings in this sample.

Conclusions

The following conclusions emerged from this chapter. First, the absence of a prior criminal record was not enough to secure a defendant's release according to this survey. It did, however, increase the possibility of ROR (151/257) and reduce the likelihood of bond (68/472). The defendants' type of release was thus contingent on other factors, the nature of the offense being most significant.

Second, there was a positive correlation between number of prior arrests and bail amount. Thirty-two

of 68 defendants (49%) with no prior arrests had bail
bond set under $500. Fifty-six of 178 defendants (31%)
with one or two arrests had bond less than $500; 62 of
213 defendants (29%) with 3 to 9 arrests had less than
$500. The figures were for cash bail and ROR, as
Table III shows.

Third, Tables IV and V showed that there was a
positive correlation between lack of supportive information and the bail amount. Two hundred eighty-
seven of 472 Probation Reports lacked necessary data
to make an objective determination more favorable to
the defendant. Table V revealed that 143 of 257
reports (55%) were similarly incomplete. The importance
of Table V as contrasted with Table IV was that it was
certain that all 257 ROR types were release only in
96 of 257 cases (36%) but the remainder were released
in spite of inadequate data or a negative report,
sustaining, again, that the nature of the offense was
the paramount factor in pretrial release.

The fact that release could be obtained without
the application of all Code criteria or denied in
spite of the fulfillment of the Code's criteria
established that all factors were not weighed equally
and some were not considered at all.

Table VI showed that being armed with a weapon
was a significant factor for only 16 of 94 cases (17%)
had bail less than $500. Table VII was comparable.
Thirty-nine of 257 ROR's (14%) were released when
weapons were an issue but 29 had to post cash bail.
The differentiation among bail types when the presence
of a weapon was involved was attributed to the nature
of the weapon. Finally, injury to the victim was not
significant in these cases. When a weapon's use led
to injury - 92 of 162 cases (57%) - 27 of the 92 were
ROR'd (29%). Injury to the victim was not significant
in the type of bail determined, whereas the presence
of a weapon was.

These conclusions affirm: first, that all
factors in the bail determination were not given equal
consideration. The nature of the offense, the prior
record and presence of a weapon were postively
correlated with the type of bail. Second, the absence
of necessary probation report data correlated posi-
tively with the type of bail. These factors of
positive correlation when compared to the negative

182

correlation of the social situation and economic situation of the defendants as seen in Chapter III and VI, revealed that the provisos for bail in criminal procedure were being selectively applied both in content and method with the result that each defendant did not have the equal protection of the law.

FOOTNOTES

1. Code of Criminal Procedure, Sections 550-556.

2. Criminal Procedure Law, Section 510.30, 2a, (v).
    P. 194.

3. See Sample

4. See Chapter III, p. 184.

5. L.T. Wilkins, Social Deviance, pp. 18-20.

6. Weber, "Sacred Law," in Charism and Institution
    Building. Chicago: University of Chicago Press,
    1968, pp. 83-87.

7. Code of Criminal Procedure, Sections 550-556.

8. C. Foote, "The Coming Constitutional Crisis in
    Bail," 113 University of Pennsylvania Law Review,
    1965, pp. 959-60.

9. E. Goffman, Stigma, New Jersey: Prentice Hall,
    1963, p. 41.

10. Criminal Procedure Law, Section 510.30, 2a, (vi).

CHAPTER VII

IMPLICATIONS OF BAIL FOR THE
CRIMINAL JUSTICE SYSTEM

Introduction

The most important change in social atmosphere was the public attitude towards this issue. First, until the mid-1950s there was little attention given to the bail phenomenon.[1] Second, an awareness of injustice or inequity in the economics of the system as it functioned had not concretized into any action programs. Third, the movement towards change in the bail system was generated by concern both within the legal profession as exemplified by the research of Caleb Foote[2] and philanthropists like Louis Schweitzer.[3] The decade of the 1960s had become the decade of awareness of the bail problem as the spate of literature on the topic, both popular and professional, indicates.[4] The major issue remains: will changes be mandated? Knowing what the problems of the bail system were and some indications of their solution, what direction will change take? The central problems were failure to receive equal treatment under law and concomitant denial of due process. The desire for change was present. The kind of changes that will solve the problems, not just ameliorate them, had not been made yet.

The challenge

The Federal Government, as a result of bail conferences in 1964[5] and 1965,[6] mandated changes in the Federal Rules of Criminal Procedure regarding bail. On June 22, 1966, Lyndon B. Johnson, then President, signed into law the revised rule 46 of the Federal Code of Criminal Procedure, Section 3146, which prohibits the denial of bail to an indigent accused.[7] Regrettably, the rule does not specify the mechanisms of non-financial pretrial release. The reasons for this are clear from this study. Non-financial mechanisms for release are easily articulated but difficult to apply.

The changes in the New York State Law governing bail, the first important changes in over fifty years, reflect the community's awareness of the bail problem. The Code of Criminal Procedure's bail provisions written in the 19th century[8] remained unchanged until The Criminal Procedure Law was effectuated on September 1, 1971.[9] The significance of the New York State change rests in the provision of a wide variety

of types of release, especially non-financial types.
Up to 1964 the choice was bail bond or jail. From 1964
to 1971 the choice was widened to include cash bail
option[10] or selective supervised release under the
aegis of the Vera Foundation.[11]

While the door to pretrial release was opened
a bit wider, the determination of criteria for release
left a great deal to be desired. The report on the
Manhattan Bail Project[12] was the first evidence of
weighted criteria for pretrial release. Patterns of
job, family and residential stability would enable
some to be released before trial who might not be able
to afford a sizeable bond. It also helped if you had
never been arrested before and the criminal act was not
terribly offensive - eliminating therefore narcotics-
related crimes, crimes of violence and sexual assaults.
The Bail Project literally fished out the milder types
and offered some route out of a detention cell for
those poorer and lower middle class types whose personal
lives and conduct were not outrageous.[13] This left the
element which could pay the high bail - the members of
syndicated crime, the affluent - and the grossest types
- the addicts, the pushers, the sexual deviates, the
repeaters, the jobless, rootless, and those without
references. The former group took care of themselves,
the latter group appeared so undesirable that they were
left to the detention cells. In New York this group
was mainly young adults between 21 and 25. Many were
addicts supporting their habit whose brushes with the
law came because of their habit or their evident social
alienation.[14] More than half of these defendants in
criminal court were black or Spanish. Clearly they
did not meet the middle-class value standards of the
Manhattan Bail Project. They were not desirable
candidates for the services of bail bondsmen[15] nor the
criminal court lawyer whose office was his briefcase
and whose business was in fees.[16] The result was an
estate system of stratification in the pretrial release
of the criminal justice system. The first estate, the
aristocrats of crime, could purchase their freedom.
The second estate, the middle class whose work habits
made them reasonable risks, were served by bail bondsmen and some projects. The third estate, street
criminal types, was left to fill the detention cells
because they had the dual handicap of penury and un-
desirability. When such a social structure evolves in
a democratic society committed to the principles of
"equal justice under law"[17] and the presumption of
innocence,[18] then the choice is clear. Design the bail

187

system to function according to the social structure of
defendant classes and give up the democratic commitments
as shibboleths, or design the system so it truly affords
"equal justice under law" without regard to social
class. The previous attempts at bail projects have
had in actuality been fishing expeditions for criteria
of bailability. The Manhattan Bail Project was
particularly concerned to avoid candidates whose
crimes involved a personal contact, involved the use
of drugs, or sexuality. They also were disinclined to
obtain release for the unemployed.[19] Bail funds[20]
arose not to attempt to deal with the criteria of
bailability but rather simply to provide the money
necessary to release those who were detained. In this
attempt many of the projects were successful, depending
upon the amount of resources available to them and the
responsibility of the subjects who were bailed. However, these approaches were essentially pragmatic,
concerned with the pretrial liberty of the defendants
rather than a constitutional or wider social implications of pretrial release in any democratized form.
The Department of Probation's ROR Division has established criteria for reportage, but based on the evidence
in Chapter VI, we observe that their findings lack
weighting and discrimination, and are decidedly incomplete.[21] Even bail projects as late as August 1972
have not addressed themselves to a comprehensive
analysis of the criteria for bailability, but rather
to the essential question of reducing crowding in the
houses of detention. While this goal is significant,
it is only a stopgap measure.[22]

The problem with the attempts to provide equal
justice under law, to date, is that there are no
established coherent, consistent instrumentalities for
the application of bail criteria. The criteria for
bail as they are written are not unreasonable.[23] There
are some elements within the bail law or procedure
which play no part in the actual decision, and should
be eliminated. These will be discussed in the ensuing
section. The criteria for bailability are unworkable
in their present form because there are no specific
rules governing their application. The result is a
rationalization for decision-making which is labeled
"judicial discretion," which is not discretion at all
but an application of the criteria based on the
gestalt.[24] Discretion, as Wilkins[25] has shown, can
only be based on full information.[26] It has been
clearly established that judges rarely have such full
information, and when they do it shows no positive

correlation to the outcome.[27] The result has been a
denial of due process of law.[28]

The Movement of the Supreme Court

The decisions of the Supreme Court in the last
generation have revealed a growing application of the
constitutional protections of the Bill of Rights to
individuals in cases against the State.[29]

In 1947, Justice Reed in Adamson vs.
California,[30] delivering the opinion of the court,
stated:

> The due process clause of the Fourteenth
> Amendment, however does not draw all the
> rights of the federal Bill of Rights
> under its protection.[31]

Yet in the decisions which flowed from the Supreme
Court in the ensuing generation, what has happened has
been precisely the incorporation of all rights of the
federal Bill of Rights under the due process clause of
the Fourteenth Amendment in regard to their application
and in regard to their applicability to the States.
In Gideon vs. Wainwright[32] the right to counsel was
affirmed. Justice Goldberg, in delivering the opinion
of the Court in Escobedo vs. Illinois[33] affirmed the
inclusionary principle:

> The critical question in this case is
> whether, under the circumstances, the
> refusal by the police to honor petitioner's
> request to consult with his lawyer during
> the course of an interrogation constitutes
> a denial of 'The Assistance of Counsel' in
> violation of the Sixth Amendment of the
> Constitution as 'made obligatory upon the
> States by the Fourteenth Amendment,'
> Gideon vs. Wainwright, and thereby renders
> inadmissible in a state criminal trial any
> incriminating statement elicited by the
> police during the interrogation.[34]

In Mapp vs. Ohio[35] the protection against unreasonable
search and seizure was affirmed. The extension of the
right to silence as stipulated in the Fifth Amendment,
"No person. . .shall be compelled in any criminal case
to be a witness against himself. . ."[36] via the Fourteenth Amendment indicates the extend of Federal concern

189

for guaranteed liberty. In Furman vs. Georgia[37] the Supreme Court applied the Eighth Amendment's protection against "cruel and unusual punishment" to the Georgia death penalty statute via the Fourteenth Amendment. What this judicial movement implied is that the due process clause of the Fourteenth Amendment applies to the States all the norms of the Bill of Rights, not solely the basic First Amendment freedoms.[38]

In 1937 Palko vs. Connecticut,[39] articulated the wider applicability of the Fourteenth Amendment protections. Such have only come to fruition as the court heard applicable cases in the ensuing four and a half decades. But it was the earliest statement of this wider application of due process. It was Cardozo who emphasized in The Nature of the Judicial Process[40] that sociological considerations had a greater role to play in the analysis of the meaning of law. These decisions established that the court had seen law not as an abstract set of rules existing independently of the society in the manner of Austin[41] and Kelsen,[42] and that the legal acts of judges were not solely shaped by the desire to maintain formal consistency within the system. This movement away from formalism in the law's understanding and interpretation was reflective of the tradition of historical jurisprudence of Friedrich von Savigny,[43] that the legal system is part of the social order.[44] It is reflective of Henry Sumner Maine's awareness that the movement from homogeneous to heterogeneous social groupings requires the active participation and consent of the governed in the judicial process.[45] This is the tradition of Pound[46] and legal realism.[47]

Any bail challenge will be based on the Fourteenth Amendment's due process clause and the Eighth Amendment's right to bail in criminal cases. The challenge would be based on data such as those used in this book; showing that denial of the right to bail was denial of equal protection of the law. The challenge could mean the end to monetary bail as discriminatory and mandating of an entirely non-financial bail system. This question must now be addressed.

Changes in the System

There can be no doubt that the Manhattan Criminal Court demonstrated its willingness to change. It adapted to cash bail, release on recognizance, and established a broader range of secured release than

190

existed prior to September 1971. These institutional
modifications were reflective of the pressure placed
upon the court by forces outside it as well as within.
They were reflective of the pragmatism of survival.
The problem with such pragmatism was that it failed to
be self reflective. It generates changes in response
to real issues such as overcrowding in detention,
awareness of impoverishment and political pressure.
The need for comprehensive orderly change in the application of bail to all defendants in criminal proceedings still remains. It is not enough simply to
elaborate the criteria for release. It is essential
to ask what these criteria mean to the defendant as
well as the court, and to delineate with some precision
how they are to be applied. What follows is an attempt
to delineate the meaning and application of these bail
criteria.

The following issues have to be confronted.
First, the right to apply for bail in all cases should
be an absolute right. The right to bail has been
traditionally applied to non-capital offenses. However,
since the death penalty has been eliminated except for
few strictly specified crimes, the distinction between
capital and non-capital offenses should be moot.
Therefore, every defendant in a criminal action has the
right to apply for bail, to a bail hearing and to a
review of its denial on written reasons. Every defendant in a criminal action should be admitted to bail
except where failure to meet the established weighted
criteria is ascertained and the denial of bail for
cause is presented in writing by the court. Second,
the application and determination of bail should be
heard in a separate court for example, Arraignment II
or the Bail Part, let us call it. The defendant who
is brought before the bench charged with a crime,
violation, misdemeanor or felony, and who pleads not
guilty, must be continued to the Bail Part. In the
Bail Part the determination of pretrial release will
be based on the rule that the only purpose of bail is
to assure the presence of the accused in the court. On
the basis that a man is innocent until proven guilty,
a man should be released on his word to return unless
the court can present evidence indicating the contrary.
The burden of such proof must be the People's.

There are many problems in establishing criteria
and ordering their weighting. First, according to the
Uniform Crime Reports, the majority of all reported
crimes are committed by persons under 25.[48] These

persons are frequently jobless, involved with drugs, and from the lower socio-economic groupings.[49] The difficulty with any set of criteria for bailability is that they reflect the values of the social class which draws up the criteria. These values are not always consonant with those of persons who appear as defendants before the bar.

We do not have the homogeneous society of Athens where an accused was bailed to three sureties,[50] nor that of 13th century England which acknowledged stratified society.[51] The problems of heterogeneity and anonymity preclude a return to formulas of a previous era.

Second, a feature of our court system which precludes pretrial release is its impersonality. Defendants are rarely, if ever, known personally to the court. And the community at large is unable to vouch for them. The individual's anonymity before the court mitigates against a pretrial release. Thus, a major factor in the creation of perspective on the defendant is the establishment of his personal and social profile as a counter-weight to the profile of the criminal law violator.

Thus, the establishment of viable, weighted criteria must be based on significant personal and social factors which transcend class peculiarities and are applicable to all defendants in a criminal proceeding relevant to their pretrial release. These factors would be the ones that bind the defendant to the community in which he resides. These are the factors which make the defendant identifiable to the court.

What are these personal factors? These factors would include the following items: With whom does the defendant reside? Does he reside with his parents and siblings, with his wife and children, friends or alone? How long has the defendant resided at his present address? Is that address a transient residence or private residence? For whom or to whom is the defendant responsible - wife, children, parent? Does that person in a responsible relationship agree to be the surety of the defendant? If so, they should have firm grounds for release. If this person in the responsible relationship will not serve as surety, or there is no person to serve as surety, then the court is responsible to look beyond the personal factors to

192

what we will call social factors which might provide an alternative mechanism for viable pretrial release.

What are these social factors? The social factors would include the following: Does the defendant belong to a rehabilitation program, hold a job, have a record of military service? Do these afford references? If not, is there any agency which will assume responsibility for this defendant? If the defendant is able to secure positive social indicators, he is eligible for some type of release, as will be shown. Having totaled the positive personal and social factors, this tally must be balanced by the negative factors of the criminal charge.

The legal factors in a criminal charge would include the following: Is the offense a felony, misdemeanor or violation? Does the defendant have a prior record of convictions? Are they for the same offense? Has he previously failed to appear in court? Does he have a warrant against him? Are there specific pertinent, aggravated circumstances?

Cancelling these negative factors against the positive factors, what balance does the defendant obtain? Is the sum total positive or negative? A socre of zero or minus would show grounds for detention. Positive points would show grounds for release as the ensuing table will delineate.

The judge will have this data before him when he is to render his bail decision. This information based on our criteria constitutes full information and would enable the judge to exercise judicial discretion. Point score does not bind the judge but enables him to decide rationally on a set of consistent data. These personal and social factors would exclude from the determination factors which clearly bear no direct correlation to appearance in court. Such extraneous considerations would include age, sex, race, wealth, life style, mental condition, the last-mentioned falling under different rules, even though it is included in the Criminal Procedure Law section on bail. And finally it would exclude prior arrests. Clearly these factors are dysfunctional and the Procedural Law would have to be changed to accommodate the new standardized procedure.

PRETRIAL RELEASE EVALUATION FLOW CHART

A. PERSONAL FACTORS   (Value: 0 to 5)

Nature of Residence	Length of Residence (½)	Type Residence Private/other (½) Yes / No	Responsible for others (½) Yes / No	Personal Surety Available (½) Yes / No	= Range
a. With parents & family: and/or	1 2 3 4 5				
b. Wife & children and/or	1 2 3 4 5				
c. With friend(s) and/or	1 2 3 4 5				
d. Alone	1 2 3 4 5	½	½ 0	½ 0	½ 0

Range 0 to 6½

Move to Social Factors

B. SOCIAL FACTORS   (Value: 0 to 5)

Community Relationship	Last 5 yrs.	References (½) Yes / No	(+ ½) Agree to Surety — Agency Surety	Points for Release
a. Membership in Program: and/or	1 2 3 4 5	Yes No		
b. Membership in Activity: and/or	1 2 3 4 5	½		
c. Employment	1 2 3 4 5	½ 0	0	
d. Military Service	1 2 3 4 5			0 to 6

Move to Legal

194

C. LEGAL FACTORS

Nature of Offense (Value -1 to -3)

Felony	-3
Misdemeanor	-2
Violation	-1

(Value -1 to -5) With Prior Convictions

1 2 3 4 5
1 2 3 4 5
1 2 3 4 5

(Value -1 to -5) Offense Same

1 2 3 4 5

(-1, 0)
Prior Failure to Appear

Yes -1
No 0

(-1, 0)
Extant Warrant

Yes -1
NO 0

(-1, 0)
Aggravated Circumstance

Injury   Property Unrecovered   Weapon

Yes No   Yes No   Yes No
-1 0   -1 0   -1 0

(-1,0)

= RANGE   1 - 18

Points Against Release

195

SCORE   TOTAL +_____

          TOTAL -_____

    IF SCORE IS:

        (1) Greater than 1/2 but less than or
             equal to 2 RECOMMEND CONDITIONAL
             RELEASE*

        (2) Greater than 2 RECOMMEND RELEASE

        (3) Zero or less RECOMMEND DETENTION

    *Conditional Release Options[51]

        1. Day release if employed

        2. Day release with project

        3. Weekend release to family

        4. Supervised release to supportive
            program

PROCEDURAL LAW

A standardized procedure such as described with a set of point values offers a consistent formula for application. It is a clear standard from which an appeal for or against release can be made by either prosecutor or defense counsel. It offers a weighting of relevant factors based on arraignment experience[52] described by Ares, Rankin and Sturz,[53] Suffet,[54] Blumberg,[55] Schaffer[56] and the author, to mention only some students in the field.

The present release system only uses points when other release possibilities such as bond or cash bail have failed. The system described above would end that discrimination and apply a uniform standard for all defendants. This standard would allow for substantive appeal based on evidence which is directly related to bail purpose, appearance. It eliminates factors which are potentially discriminatory - age, sex, race, prior arrest record, and conflicting class values over occupation or life style. The difference of the standardized format described above from the formulations of other bail groups is that this formulation must apply across the board to all defendants and it removes the necessity for wealth which is totally irrelevant to appearance. It requires additional revisions in the bail procedure both eliminating vague factors such as criminal record and mental condition, and incorporating the format for weighting the factors delineated which will indicate likelihood of appearance. These recommendations would give greater assurance of due process, afford the equal protection of the law and demonstrate that release pending trial would not be based excessively on any one factor.

FOOTNOTES

1. Dorothy Tompkins. Bail in the United States: A
   Bibliography. Berkeley, Calif.: Institute of
   Governmental Studies, 1964.

2. Caleb Foote. "A Study of the Administration of
   Bail in New York City." Vol. 106, University of
   Pennsylvania Law Review, No. 5, 1958, p. 693.

3. Louis Schweitzer, founded the Vera Institute of
   Justice. See on this Bail and Summons: 1965,
   Washington, D.C.: Vera Institute of Justice, 1966,
   Introduction.

4. See Bibliography.

5. The National Conference on Bail and Criminal
   Justice. Proceedings and Interim Report. 1965.
   New York: The Institute on the Operation of
   Pretrial Release Projects, 1966.

6. Bail and Summons: 1965, op. cit., "Introduction."

7. Ibid., p. xxvi.

8. The Code of Criminal Procedure. Albany, N.Y.:
   The State Legislature, 1886.

9. The Criminal Procedure Law of New York. Irving
   Shapiro, editor. New York: Gould Publications,
   1971. Part 3, Title P, Article 510, Section 30.

10. The 1972 Criminal Justice Plan. New York:
    Executive Committee on the Criminal Justice
    Coordinating Council, 1972, pp. 73-78.

11. Ares, Rankin and Sturz. "The Manhattan Bail
    Project: An Interim Report on the Use of Pre-
    trial Parole." New York University Law Review,
    Vol. 38, January 1963, pp. 67-95.

12. Loc. cit.

13. Hans Zeisel. "Methodological Problems and Techniques in Sociological Research." Law and Society Review, Vol. 2, No. 3, May 1968, pp. 504-508. See also "The Marginal Middle Class: A Reconsideration," by Richard F. Hamilton, The American Sociological Review, Vol. 31, No. 2, April 1966, pp. 192-199.

14. Charles Reich. "The Law and the Corporate State," in Sociological Readings in the Conflict Perspective, edited by William Chambliss. Massachusetts: Addison Wesley Publishing Co., 1973, pp. 445-454.

15. Vide supra, Chapter III, footnote 70.

16. Abraham S. Blumberg. "The Practice of Law as Confidence Game: Organizational Cooptation of a Profession." In Crime and the Legal Process, edited by William Chambliss. New York: McGraw Hill, 1968, pp. 220-236.

17. The Fourteenth Amendment to the Constitution of the United States, in Appendix B, in Lockhart, Kamisar and Choper, Constitutional Rights and Liberties. St. Paul, Minn.: The West Publishing Co., 1970, p. 22.

18. The presumption of innocence concept is found in Stack vs. Boyle 342 U.S. 1. 4 (1951).

19. The Criminal Procedure Law, Article 510.30.

20. See Chapter I, footnotes 78 and 79.

21. See Chapter VI, Tables IV and V.

22. Cynthia Wainwright. Department of Correction Bail Reevaluation Project Final Report. New York: The Fund for the City of New York, August 31, 1972, p. ii. See also, page 1.

23. The Criminal Procedure Law, Article 510.30.

24. Edwin M. Schur. Law and Society: A Sociological View. New York: Random House, 1968, pp. 46 and 47.

25. Leslie T. Wilkins. Social Deviance. New Jersey: Prentice Hall, 1964, pp. 44-45. See also pp. 17-19.

26. See Chapter VI, Tables IV and V.

27. See Chapter IV, Summary and Conclusions. See also Chapter V, Tables I, II and Chapter VI, Conclusions.

28. Caleb Foote. "The Coming Constitutional Crisis in Bail." 113 University of Pennsylvania Law Review (1965), Part 2, p. 1151.

29. Lockhart, Kamisar and Choper, op. cit., Chapter V.

30. Adamson vs. California in Lockhart, Kamisar and Choper, pp. 141-146.

31. Lockhart, Kamisar and Choper, op. cit., p. 142.

32. Gideon vs. Wainwright 372 U.S. 335 (1963).

33. Escobedo vs. Illinois 378 U.S. 478 (1964).

34. Escobedo in Lockhart, Kamisar and Choper, op. cit., pp. 252-258.

35. Mapp vs. Ohio in Lockhart, Kamisar and Choper, op. cit., pp. 177-184.

36. Fifth Amendment to the Constitution of the United States, Appendix B in Lockhart, Kamisar and Choper, op. cit., p. 19.

37. Furman vs. Georgia in New York Times, June 30, 1972, p. 1.

38. Palko vs. Connecticut, in Lockhart, Kamisar and Choper, op. cit., p. 140.

30. Ibid., p. 141.

40. Benjamin Cardozo. The Nature of the Judicial Process. Lecture 3.

41. John Austin. The Province of Jurisprudence
    Determined and the Use of the Study of Juris-
    prudence. Edited with an introduction by H.L.A.
    Hart. London: Weidenfield and Nicholson, 1955.

42. Schur. Law and Society: A Sociological View,
    pp. 27 and 28.

43. Friedrich von Savigny. "Of the Vocation of Our
    Age for Legislation and Jurisprudence." In Cohen
    and Cohen, eds., Readings in Jurisprudence and
    Legal Philosophy. New Jersey: Englewood Cliffs,
    Prentice-Hall, 1951, p. 388.

44. Schur, op. cit., p. 30.

45. Henry S. Maine. Ancient Law. London: J. Murray,
    1863, p. 3.

46. Roscoe Pound. The Scope and Subject Matter of
    Law, III. In Jurisprudence, 5 Vols., pp. 289-
    350.

47. Wilfred E. Rumble. "Legal Realism, Sociological
    Jurisprudence and Mr. Justice Holmes." Journal
    of the History of Ideas, Vol. 26, October-
    December 1965, pp. 547-66.

48. The Uniform Crime Reports, 1979. Washington,
    D.C.: The Department of Justice.

49. See Chapter IV, Tables II, III and V; Chapter V,
    Tables II, III and V.

50. "The prosecutor in a murder-charge must at once
    demand bail from the defendant and the latter
    shall provide three substantial sureties - as
    approved by the court or the judges in such cases
    - who guarantee to produce him at the trial, and
    if a man be unwilling to . . .provide these
    sureties the court must take, bind and keep him,
    and produce him at the trial of the case." 2
    Plato Laws, 261. Burry Edition, 1952. See also
    Harrison, The Law of Athens. Procedure. Oxford:
    Clarendon Press, 1971.

51. Henri Pirenne. _Economic and Social History of Medieval Europe_. New York: Harcourt Brace and World, Inc., a Harvest Book, 1937, Part 2, The Towns; Subsection 3, Urban Institutions and the Law, pp. 49-56; and Part 3, Land and the Rural Classes; Subsection 1, Manorial Organization and Serfdom, pp. 57-65. See also G.G. Coulton, _Medieval Village, Manor and Monastery_, New York: Harper and Brothers, Harper Torch Books, 1960 (original edition 1925), Chapter 14, "Legal Barriers to Enfranchisement," pp. 166-177.

52. Wainwright, _op. cit._, p. 5, p. 22, p. 24, p. 26.

53. Ibid., p. 26, Appendix A.

54. "The Manhattan Bail Project," _loc cit._

55. Suffet. "Bail Setting. A Study of Courtroom Interaction." _Loc cit._ See also by Suffet, "Patterns of Failure to Raise Bail." Unpublished manuscript, Vera Foundation, 1965.

56. Abraham S. Blumberg. _Criminal Justice_. Chicago: Quadrangle Books, 1968, Chapter 3.

57. Andrew Schaffer. "The Problem of Overcrowding in the Detention Institutions of New York City: An Analysis of Causes and Recommendations for Alleviation." Mimeograph. _A Report to the Mayor's Criminal Justice Coordinating Council_. New York: Vera Institute of Justice, January 1969, pp. 30-34. See also _. . .and Justice for All_. A Report of the Temporary Commission on the State Court System, January 1973. Three Parts. See especially Chapter I, "Summary of Recommendations," pp. 7-17, and Part 2, Chapter VI, "Releasing, Detaining and Indicting Criminal Defendants," pp. 65-77.

Historically, bail arose in response to the problems of detention before trial.[1] The situation has now reversed itself where bail has been used as an instrument of preventive detention. The two decades from 1960 to 1980 have shown the disabling and questionable nature of such a marginally legal practice as "excessive bail" in lieu of pretrial release but such abuses do not constitute a justification for preventive detention. Such an argument must be made in its own right.

The movement in the 1980s in criminal justice is to set forth preventive detention statutes which will enable jurisdictions to deny pretrial freedom to certain offenders for specifically enumerated offenses. Constitutionally, as has been seen earlier,[2] the only requirement is that bail shall not be excessive and statutorily that the defendant agree to appear when required. The criteria for evaluating these determinations have been the stumbling blocks.[3] Increasingly, jurisdictions are including the potential dangerousness of the offender as a criterion for preventive detention. The dilemma with such a criterion as with those applicable to bail is that there is no certainty that the criteria in either situation, when applied, are purposive. As the lack of weighted measures to determine likelihood of appearance has left the courts to invoke them or not as they see fit,[4] so the prediction of dangerousness is equally uncertain. The political and social climate of dissatisfaction with the pretrial process has led to calls for preventive detention.

Are additional safeguards needed? While the public fear of crime has grown and the reportage on violence responds to this popular fear, what should constitute preventive detention is speculative. The following arguments pro and con are set forth to pose the questions rather than offer solutions.

The case for preventive detention

The issue of dangerousness has always existed just below the surface of the bail decision process.[5] There always has been a question of how does one balance the payment of money against the presence of an atrocity. How much is enough? In the purview of the Founding Fathers in 1789 most crimes were serious and

serious crimes were not considered bailable. Once
serious crimes were separated from "capital" crimes the
issue of statutory bailment was broached.

Procedural due process is concerned with the
issue of predictability: 1) predictability of appearance
when required by the court; 2) predictability of likelihood of recidivation while on bail; 3) predictability
of dangerousness. Bail addresses itself to the first
question, essentially.

The District of Columbia Criminal Code Title 22
at 1321 places particular emphasis on two and three
above. It also considers second offenders and parolees
as presumptively dangerous. There is a sixty day limit
on such presumptions during which time a hearing must
be held. The District of Columbia has averaged twenty
five such cases per year in a process that is cumber-
some and highly litigious. The Omnibus Crime Control
and Safe Streets Act of 1968 and the 1981 Attorney
General's Task Force Report on Violent Crime argue for
more restrictive release. Senate Bill S.1554 cosponsor-
ed by Senators Strom Thurmond and Edward Kennedy would
permit judges to consider potential dangerousness. The
Federal Rules of Criminal Procedure, Section 3146 at 46
could be amended for this provision. The dilemma remains, however. What constitutes a reasonable measure
of dangerousness? Is it the defendant arrested for
assault with a deadly weapon, with three arrests and
one conviction? Is a deadly weapon only a firearm or
coult it be a motor vehicle operated by a drunk?

While New York has no preventive detention
statute comparable to the District of Columbia (1970)
Section 510.30 of the Criminal Procedure Law does allow
for potential dangerousness as an evaluative criterion
for pretrial release.[6] The Mayor's Survey of the
Criminal Justice System: Report and Recommendations,
New York: 250 Broadway, January 1981 argues for more
restrictive provisions for pretrial release.[7] According
to Mayor Koch

> Studies have shown that judges have often
> set excessively high bail or ordered
> individuals imprisoned who are likely,
> according to statistical analyses, to
> reappear. The unspoken--and I believe
> legitimate--concern is that the defend-
> ant with a violent criminal history, or
> one who has committed a particularly

heinous crime, or who has a long list of
pending cases, will present a threat to
the well-being of the community if
released. It is time that this very
real concern is addressed by responsible
legislation that openly addresses the
problem.[8]

The Mayor then goes on to set forth the criteria for
dangerousness that would warrant detention. These are:
1) murder in the first or second degree and kidnapping;
first degree arson or manslaughter; 2) a violent felony
charge with a prior violent felony offense within the
last 10 years and 3) if charged with a felony while
awaiting trial on a felony.[9] Evaluation of individual
circumstances, likelihood of indictment being known
within 72 hours, and a ninety day trial rule would be
controlling factors.

According to Judge Herbert I. Altman of Criminal
Court in New York County

I have seen literally hundreds of defendants
who were held on bail in serious felony
cases released three days later because
of unreasonable time limitations. Needless
to say, I would suggest that CPL 180.80 be
amended to . . .extend the time limitation
from 72 hours to five court days.[9]

Mayor Koch would also propose legislation to allow five
days to act upon a felony complaint in cases where the
defendant is in custody. This is similar to the requirements of Section 170.70 of the Criminal Procedure
Law in misdemeanor cases.

The Attorney General's Task Force on Violent
Crime offers the following criteria as evaluative of
presumptive dangerousness. First, there must be some
evidence of dangerousness. What that evidence is would
have to be assessed on a case by case basis and be
reasonable. Second, a judge can deny pretrial release
when no amount of money would assure appearance. The
Drug Enforcement Administration has a large number of
bail jumpers from high bail because the stakes are high,
money is plentiful so the loss of a million dollars in
cash in a multimillion dollar business is a pittance.
Clearly the issue of likelihood of appearance in such
cases weighs heavily against the defendant in as many

206

as 1700 out of 7000 cases annually according to the Drug Enforcement Administration.

Third, a judge may presume to deny pretrial release to anyone who has committed a crime while on bail. Such a presumptive denial might be viable over a defined time span, for example five years. It appears that approximately 25% of all bailed defendants are rearrested while on bail. Fourth, a prosecutor may appeal a bail decision. Certainly, it has been the argument in this book that the right to bail, statutorily, should be based on clear criteria fairly applied.[10] It makes sense in light of the current controversy, to make the application for bail an open hearing in court with argument presented by both sides and the judge ruling in writing.[11] Issues of dangerousness in bail and detention proceedings would be a matter of record and appealed if necessary as the Task Force recommends.

It is necessary to develop a body of case law on these procedural matters through the appellate process. The Nebraska case, Parker v Roth[12] in which bail was denied in a forceable rape case, decided on November 7, 1978 that an amendment to the Nebraska Constitution to deny bail in such cases was constitutional.[13] The case was appealed to the Supreme Court of the United States and certiorari was denied.[14] However in 1980 the Supreme Court agreed to hear the case.[15] The case was argued on January 18, 1982 and in March the Court declared the issue moot as the defendant was convicted and imprisoned for the offense. The Court did leave the door ajar for future litigation by noting that a class action suit might have been more appropriate. However, this illustration presents evidence of the difficulty in trying to build a body of case law on the issue of preventive detention.[16]

Alternatives to preventive detention do exist in career criminal projects, major offense bureau prosecutions and revocation of bail or parole for those arrested while on release. The use of wealth as a weapon to hold suspects is not a healthy practice as it is fraught with too many due process risks. One of the arguments against preventive detention is the call for a speedy trial. Speedy trial is not an argument for or against preventive detention as the fact that one may be detained for whatever reason is not mitigated by the brevity of the experience. Speedy trial is an argument for reduction in recidivation while on bail, if cases are brought to trial in less than ninety days.[17]

The case against preventive detention

The arguments against preventive detention lack some of the persuasiveness of the proponents' position. The opponents of preventive detention face the difficulty of convincing the public that a defendant burdened by an apparent factual presumption of guilt is entitled to the procedural presumption of innocence under our due process system of justice. The difficulties lie in the public's fear of criminals, a sense that the law "coddles" criminals and a sense that factual presumption of guilt obviates the necessity for much of this due process "nonsense." This last attitude is rooted in an a-historical sense that the long history of denial of due process in colonial America which was persuasive for the Founding Fathers is any longer relevant. Such abstract reasoning neglects the point that those due process guarantees stand with each of us in the unlikely event that they might be needed like the irrelevant seat belt until the moment of impact. While statutes can mandate the wisdom of protecting ourselves by restraint, or the purchase of auto insurance we may never use, these same statutes cannot prevent us from acting against our own best interests. The risks run in opting for preventive detention are similar.

The arguments for societal safety are persuasive. The dangers in supporting that argument seem to be nil. However, the implied risks in waiving the due process protections are not unlike taking the risk of driving without a seat belt. It may not matter until it happens to oneself.

The argument can be made, certainly, that preventive detention violates the spirit of The Constitution of the United States. The long history of abuses of authority since the English Renaissance were important to the Founding Fathers. These abuses, well documented elsewhere, included: star chamber proceedings, detention at the King's pleasure in the Tower of London or elsewhere for political reasons, without charge. This abuse led to The Habeas Corpus Act of 1679. Detention for religious and political beliefs and related abuses were explicitly rejected in The Bill of Rights in 1789.

The greatest difficulty as has been seen in Chapters III, IV and V is the failure of predictive mechanisms. There is a complete absence of justification for preventive detention. Among the unresolved issues in the matter of preventive detention are: first, how does the presumptive dangerousness affect outcome? Second, will a defendant, innocent until proven guilty, but labelled dangerous, experience any overt or covert bias in the prosecution of his case? Third, how will the stigma of dangerousness affect an acquitted defendant?

The National Bureau of Standards study mentioned earlier indicated a low base rate of violent crime, 15%, of those out on bail between arraignment and conviction. There is no workable predictive mechanism to determine dangerousness in that sequence of events between arraignment and disposition. Theoretically, if 150 out of 1000 defendants recidivate, to determine which 150 out of 1000 will recidivate with a 70% reliability or 105 offenders, it would be necessary to detain an additional 255 defendants who would not recidivate. To hypothesize a 100% accurate predictor, a much larger population would have to be presumptively detained.

What becomes clear under this modality of social defense policy is that the system imposes punishment or a penalty in advance of proof. There is no prima facie case for dangerousness. If a defendant is presumed dangerous can the deprivation of pretrial liberty exclude treatment for the presumed dangerousness?[18]

Shall such presumptive detention be viewed as retributive and as a statement of general deterrence policy or exemplary punishment? The argument can be made that a defendant detained in advance on grounds of dangerousness or possible flight is punished in advance and this is comparable to an indeterminate sentence.[19]

Among the anomalies of the preventive detention thesis is the question of what to do with the dangerous offender in preventive detention who is acquitted. Having labelled this defendant dangerous should he be let go upon acquittal?

Clearly there should be no punishment without proof of guilt beyond a reasonable doubt, established

by due process. Otherwise our judicial system takes on
the trappings of a repressive regime where the burden
of proof for release falls upon the defendant rather
than the burden of proof for restraint being laid at
the feet of the state. As we have seen in the human
rights struggle and the detention of dissidents such
as Sharansky in the U.S.S.R. such preventive detention
systems are fraught with areas for abuse.

Alternatives to preventive detention

What alternatives exist in preventive detention?
First, under the usual criminal procedure, speedy
trial would reduce the likelihood of recidivation
dramatically, but not the stigma of being labelled
dangerous. Second, certain punishment with specific
incarceration may be deterring. However, society can
hardly opt for preventive detention at the same time
it is defeating a prison bond issue. Third, better
pro-active neighborhood policing, community anti-crime
programs, tenant patrols, block watchers and senior
citizen protective services would be supporting as it
is clearly impossible to rely on police personnel to
be the first line of defense in preventing serious
crime. Fourth, better prosecution management systems
for cases would assure the proper movement of serious
offender cases by Management Information Systems to
trial and disposition as is done in Major Offense
Bureau cases.

Analogous to the Founding Fathers view of all
crime as serious, today it might be argued that all
crime is dangerous to the fabric of our society but
there is a variance of degree. Whether one approaches
dangerousness as a function of the offense, as the
Classical School of Criminology might, or as a condition of the offender, as the Positivists would, there
is still an obligation to determine what we mean by
dangerousness. An unscrupulous nursing home operator
who deprives elderly patients of services and defrauds
them of their worldly goods may be much more dangerous
to society than the "push in" robber who assaults the
elderly. If violence is our sole criterion we may be
missing the point.

Correspondingly, the determination of dangerousness must be defined in either forensic or behavioral
terms. Until it is established whether the defendant's

dangerousness is forensic, i.e., rooted in some psychological or pathological condition which might remove the defendant from the realm of criminal liability or until society decides that certain behaviors are defined as more or less dangerous than others it seems impossible to administer a preventive detention statute.

Federal and state law must risk the articulation of dangerousness and preventive detention openly by statute. The only hope to arrive at some possible consensus is in the development of a body of case law based upon the challenges to extant statutes. The limits of this approach have been noted earlier. One could reject the preventive detention thesis entirely.

Finally, it comes down to the question on which side shall the risk of harm be taken. For the last two hundred years we have stated clearly that society must take the risk on behalf of all those accused in a due process model of justice. The balance is now shifting wherein society is demanding that the accused take the risk on behalf of society. Should we as a nation decide that it is in our national interest to move more in the direction of social defense policy in the administration of criminal justice that is a much larger issue than preventive detention. However preventive detention may simply be the first in a series of issues moving us in that direction.

Certainly it should not be argued that the abuse of the bail privilege is a rationale for its removal and replacement by preventive detention.

Footnotes

1. See Chapter I.

2. See Chapter II.

3. See Chapters III, IV, V.

4. <u>People</u> v. <u>Edmond</u> 266 NW 3nd 640 App. 1978 in
   Kusnet and Benton eds. <u>Criminal Law Digest</u>
   New York: Warren, Gorham and Lamont, 1981,
   rev. ed. 1981 Cumulative Supplement No. 2. 94.

5. <u>Criminal Procedure Law</u> Part P. Section 510.30
   note 6, p. 19.

6. Ibid., note 6. See also Section 530.60 (2) (a).

7. <u>Mayor's Survey of the Criminal Justice System</u>:
   <u>Report and Recommendations</u>, New York:
   250 Broadway, January 1981.

8. Ibid., pp. 3-22.

9. Ibid., pp. 3-23.

10. See note 4.

11. See Chapter III

12. 202 Nebraska 850, 278 N.W. 3nd 106, 117.

13. Article 1, Section 9, 1978.

14. 444 U.S. 920 (1979).

15. "Justices to Study Denial of Bail on Sex Violence,"
    <u>The New York Times</u>, October 6, 1981.

16. U.S. Sup. Ct. 80-2165.

17. See National Bureau of Standards Study infra.

18. <u>Bell</u> v. <u>Wolfish</u> 441 U.S. 520, 47 L.W. 4507.

19. <u>Curbing The Career Criminal: A Progress Report</u>,
    New York: The Citizens Crime Commission,
    April 1982, Part II.

CHAPTER IX

CONCLUSION

The evidence from empirical data on the application of New York State's procedural laws on bail and constitutional law indicates that the present bail system is inconsistent in its application of the bail criteria. The criteria for bailability need to be reexamined for their applicability. The purpose of bail is to assure the appearance of the defendant when required. Criteria productive of appearance should be the only criteria.

First, money bail in any form does not per se guarantee the appearance of the defendant. It also divides the defendants into economic classes -- those who can afford bail and those who cannot. This suggests a constitutional discrimination by denial of equal protection of the law due to lack of funds.

The mental condition of a defendant cannot be evaluated at a bail proceeding. It is also beyond the judge's professional competence. Such questions should be decided by experts outside the court on referral. This criterion should be eliminated.

The defendant's employment shows no positive correlation with his suitability for bail. It should be eliminated because it sets up a criterion which is artificial and in no way evidencing that the defendant will return.

The defendant's family ties or dependents bear significant relationship to his release only insofar as a family member will assure the court of the defendant's return. Criteria relevant to this assurance should be developed on the English model.

The defendant should be released to any reliable sponsoring agency, person or group which agrees to his supervision regardless of the nature of the offense. Naturally there may be cases where no reliable sureties will be found. This provides an indicator of what crimes society refuses to accede to the bail request and allows society to take its share in the control of defendants. It is important to note that groups already exist to perform this service.

When a defendant in a criminal action has found no party to offer surety, he still has the right to apply for bail based on social indicators of his reliability -- his residence, his good record, his community base and references. These weighted positive factors should be counterbalanced by the weighted negative factors of nature of offense, record of convictions - not arrests, prior failures to appear, warrants and aggravated circumstances.

The present failure of the administration of bail in Criminal Court in New York County is that it lacks weighted criteria for judgment of suitability for release. It has been shown that ROR point system is utilized inadequately and prejudicially. The court has no way to know if the Probation Department really sought the data required. The evidence indicates it does not.

The court has established a pretrial services section for victims and witnesses. Indigent defendants learn to prepare their cases. This should continue to include legal counsel, access to bail criteria information and available means to meet them, such as telephones for those detained. The successful application for release pending trial should be circumscribed by rules which the defendant, his surety if any, must meet. These may include counseling, use of social, medical and psychiatric services.

Finally, the court's decision to release or detain a defendant should be written and based on the use of weighted criteria informing judicial discretion. The ultimate responsibility for the decision is the judge's. He may wish others to share it with him but it is constitutionally his prerogative which he may not give over to another. The written decision should contain the judge's reasons pro or con and be subject to appeal by defense or prosecution, and review by a superior judge within 72 hours, not simply by the same judge or day later.

Bail release cannot be isolated from other procedures, especially a speedy trial. The evidence is clear and irrefutable that the prompt administration of justice reduces the danger of violation of conditions of release and is more equitable to defendant and plaintiff. It also assures the availability of a larger pool of agents for surety when cases do not become protracted.

This book does not address itself to the detention of witnesses or post-trial release. It would seem that logically the same rules should apply with latitude for some peculiarities such as safety of witnesses. Obviously such issues should mandate a detention system which is far different from a system of imprisonment for the convicted. Clearly this remains to be done.

BIBLIOGRAPHY

Advisory Committee on Pretrial Proceedings. American
    Bar Association, Standards Relating to Pretrial
    Release. Chicago: American Bar Association,
    1968.

"Aid Will Revise Court Scheduling." The New York
    Times, Sunday, November 8, 1970.

Annual Report. New York: Department of Correction,
    1969.

Ares, C.E., Rankin, A. and Sturz, H. "The Manhattan
    Bail Project: An Interim Report on the Use of
    Pre-Trial Parole." New York University Law
    Review, 38 January 1962, pp. 67-95.

_____and Sturz, H. "Bail and the Indigent Accused."
    Crime and Delinquency, 8:12-20, January 1962.

"Arrest Reforms Sought in Canada." The New York
    Times, Sunday, June 14, 1970.

Austin, John. The Province of Jurisprudence
    Determined and the Use of the Study of Juris-
    prudence, ed. with introduction by H.L.A. Hart.
    London: Weidenfield and Nicolson, 1955.

"Awaiting Their Day in Court." The New York Times,
    Sunday, December 6, 1970.

"Bail: An Ancient Practice Reexamined." 70 Yale Law
    Journal, 1961, pp. 966-977 (Appendix: State Laws
    Governing the Right to Bail.)

"Bail: Justice Far From All." New York Times
    Magazine, August 19, 1962, pp. 13ff.

"The Bail Bond Scandal." The Saturday Evening Post,
    June 20, 1964.

The Bail Reform Act. An Analysis Proposed, Amendments
    and an Alternative. Washington: American
    Enterprise Institute for Public Policy Research,
    1969.

Beeley, Arthur L. The Bail System in Chicago. The
     University of Chicago Press, 1965 (original,
     1927).

Bellamy et al v. The Judges and Justices Authorized to
     Sit in the New York City Criminal Court
     Plaintiffs' Memorandum. New York: Doubleday
     Anchor, 1960.

Bennett, James V. I Chose Prison. New York: Knopf,
     1970.

Bierstedt, Robert. "An Analysis of Social Power."
     American Sociological Review, Vol. 15, December
     1950, pp. 730-738.

Blau, Peter. Dynamics of Bureaucracy. Chicago:
     University of Chicago Press, 1955.

_____. Bureaucracy in Modern Society. New York:
     1956.

Bloomfield, Morton W. "Beowulf, Byrhtnoth, and the
     Judgment of God: Trial by Combat in Anglo-Saxon
     England." Speculum, Vol. XLIV, No. 4, October
     1969, pp. 545-559.

Blumberg, Abraham S. The Criminal Court: An
     Organizational Analysis. New York: New
     School for Social Research, Doctoral Dissertation,
     1965.

_____. "The Practice of Law as Confidence Game:
     Organizational Cooptation of a Profession." In
     Crime and the Legal Process, edited by W.J.
     Chambliss. New York: McGraw Hill, 1968, pp.
     220-236.

_____. "The Problem of Objectivity in Judicial
     Decision-Making." Social Forces, September 1967.

Botein, Bernard. "The Manhattan Bail Project: Its
     Impact on Criminology and the Criminal Law
     Process." Texas Law Review, February 1965,
     p. 391f.

Bottomley, Keith. Parole, The American Experience.
     Cambridge: Cambridge University, Doctoral
     Dissertation, unpublished, 1971.

Boulding, Kenneth E. Conflict and Defense: A General Theory. New York: Harper and Brothers, 1962.

Boyle, James B. "Case Notes," New York Law School Law Review, Vol. 26 (Winter 1981), pp. 341-65 /Bell v Wolfish 441 U.S. 520 (1979)/

Bracton, H. On the Laws and Customs of England. Translated and edited by Samuel H. Thorne. Cambridge: Harvard University Press, 1968, 2 volumes.

Bryce, James. Studies in History and Jurisprudence. Freeport, N.Y.: Books for Libraries Press, 1968, 2 volumes (original 1901).

"Burger Tells Nation's Bar to Tighten Self-Discipline." The New York Times, Tuesday, July 6, 1971.

Cardozo, Benjamin. The Nature of the Judicial Process. New Haven: Yale University Press, 1921.

"Carey signs bill to revoke bail in felony cases" New York Law Journal, July 30, 1981, Vol. 185, p. 1.

Carlin, Jerome. Lawyers' Ethics. New York: Russell Sage Foundation, 1966.

Castle, Stephen C. "Trends restricting the right to bail: the constitutionality of pre-trial detention in non-capital offenses. Criminal Justice Journal, Vol. 3 (Spring 1980), pp. 433-450.

Cavan, Ruth S. Criminology. New York: Thomas Y. Crowell, 3rd ed., 1962.

Chambliss, William. "A Sociological Analysis of the Law of Vagrancy." In Quinney, ed. Crime and Justice in Society. Boston: Little Brown, 1969, pp. 55-68.

Civil Practice Laws and Rules. Vol. 7B, Sections 6115-18. McKinney's Consolidated Laws of New York, Brooklyn, N.Y.: Edward Thompson, 1963.

Clark, Ramsey. _Crime in America_. New York: Simon and Shuster, 1970.

Coco, Joseph A. "Choice of Law in Federal Bail Abstracts: Protecting Principles of Federalism." _Fordham Law Review_, Vol. 49 (October 1980), pp. 133-155.

Code of Criminal Procedure. Vol. 66 in _McKinney's Consolidated Laws of New York_. Brooklyn, N.Y.: Edward Thompson, 1968 ed.

Cohen, Felix S. _The Legal Conscience. Selected Papers of Felix S. Cohen_, ed. by L.K. Cohen, Forward by F. Frankfurter, Intro by E.V. Rostow. New Haven, Conn.: Yale University Press, 1960.

Cohen, Morris R. _Law and the Social Order_. New York: Harcourt Brace and Co., 1933.

_____ and Felix S. eds. _Readings in Jurisprudence and Legal Philosophy_. Englewood Cliffs, N.J.: Prentice Hall, 1951.

Coke, Sir Edward. _A Little Treatise of Baile and Maineprize_. London: William Cook, 1637.

Commonwealth v. _Baker_ 343 Mass. 162.

Coser, Louis. _The Function of Social Conflict_. New York: Free Press, 1956.

Covington v. _Harris_ 419 F 2nd D.C. Circuit (1969).

"Criminal Law and its Administration." _Columbia University Law Review_, Vol. 66, No. 1, January 1966.

Criminal Procedure Law of New York. Irving Shapiro, ed. New York: Gould Publications, 1971.

"Crisis in the Courts." _The New York Times_, October 18, 1970.

Dahrendorf, Ralf. _Class and Class Conflict in Industrial Society_. Stanford: Stanford University Press, 1959.

220

_____. "Out of Utopia: Toward a Reorientation in Sociological Analysis." American Journal of Sociology, Vol. 64, September 1958, pp. 115-127.

Davis, F.J. "Law as a Type of Social Control." In Davis, Foster, Jeffrey and Davis, Society and the Law. New York: Free Press of Glencoe, 1962.

De Haas, Elsa. Antiquities of Bail; Origins and Historical Development in Criminal Cases to the Year 1275. New York: Columbia University Press, 1940.

"Delivery System Analysis of Santa Clara County, California" U.S. Department of Justice, LEAA National Institute of Law Enforcement and Criminal Justice: The Lazar Institute, Washington, D.C., 1979.

Dicey, A.V. Lectures on the Relation Between Law and Public Opinion in England in the Nineteenth Century. 2nd Edition. Preface by E.O.S. Wade. London: Macmillan, 1963 (Reprint).

Draper v. Washington, 9L.ed 2nd 974 March 18, 1972.

Durkheim, Emile. The Division of Labor in Society. New York: Free Press, 1960 (1893).

3 Edward 1 c. 15 Statutes of Westminster I, 1275.

Ehrlich, Eugen. The Fundamental Principles of the Sociology of Law. Trans. W. Moll. Cambridge: Harvard University Press, 1936. (Original 1913).

Enslein, P.T. "Prediction of Court Appearance--A Study of Bail on Cleveland. Cleveland State Law Review, Vol. 27 (1978), pp. 587-617.

Erikson, Kai. "Notes on the Sociology of Deviance." Social Problems, Vol. 9, Spring 1962, pp. 307-14.

Ervin, Sam J. "Preventive Detention: An Empirical Analysis." Harvard Civil Rights and Civil Liberties Review, Vol. 6, No. 3, March 1971, pp. 291ff.

Escobedo v. Illinois 378 U.S. 478 (1964)

Etzioni, Amitai. A Comparative Analysis of Complex
    Organizations. New York: Free Press of Glencoe,
    1961.

_____. "Two Approaches to Organizational Analysis:
    A Critique and a Suggestion." Administrative
    Science Quarterly, September 1960, pp. 257-278.

Evan, William N., ed. Law and Sociology, Exploratory
    Essays. New York: Free Press, 1962.

_____ and Levin, Ezra G. "Status-Set and Role-Set,
    Conflicts of the Stockbroker: A Problem in the
    Sociology of Law." Social Forum, Vol. 45, No. 1,
    September 1966.

Ex Parte Milburn 34 U.S. 704 (1835)

Fabricant. "Bail as a Preferred Freedom and the
    Future of New York's Revision." 18 Buffalo Law
    Review, 1969.

"Federal Advisors Study Court Load." New York Times,
    January 2, 1971.

Flemming, R.B., Kohfeld, C.W.; Uhlman, T.M. "Limits
    of Bail Reform: A Quasi-Experimental Analysis."
    Law and Society Review, Vol. 14, No. 4 (Summer
    1980), pp. 947-976.

Foote, Caleb. "The Bail System and Equal Justice."
    Federal Probation, 23 September 1959, pp. 43-48.

_____. "The Coming Constitutional Crisis in Bail."
    113, University of Pennsylvania Law Review, 1965,
    Nos. 1 and Nos. 2, pp. 959-1199.

_____. "A Study of the Administration of Bail in
    New York City." 106 University of Pennsylvania
    Law Review, No. 5, 1958, p. 653ff.

_____, Markle, J.P. and Wooley, E.A. "Compelling
    Appearance in Court: Administration of Bail in
    Philadelphia." University of Pennsylvania Law
    Review, 102, June 1954, pp. 1031ff.

Frank, Jerome. Courts on Trial. New York: Atheneum,
    1963.

Frazier, Charles E., Bock, E. Wilbur, and Henretta, John C. "Pretrial Release and Bail Decisions: The Effects of Legal, Community and Personal Variables." Criminology, Vol. 18 (August 1980), pp. 162-181.

Freed, Daniel J. and Wald, Patricia M. Bail in the United States: 1964. Washington, D.C.: National Conference on Bail and Criminal Justice.

"Freedom at a Price. Bail Bondsmen Wield Surprising Power, Stir Growing Controversy." The Wall Street Journal, Thursday, October 7, 1971, p. 1.

Friedland, Martin L. Detention Before Trial: A Study of Criminal Cases in the Toronto Magistrates Courts. Toronto: University of Toronto Press, 1965.

Friedman, Wolfgang. "Limits of Judicial Lawmaking and Prospective Overruling." Modern Law Review, Vol. 29, No. 6, November 1966.

"Gamelyn." In Middle English Verse Romances, Donald B. Sands, ed. New York: Holt, Rinehart and Winston, Inc., 1966, pp. 154-181.

Ganong, Cary, Kierstead and Pearce. Law and Society. Homewood, Ill.: Erwin, 1965.

Geis , G. "Sociology, Criminology and Criminal Law." Social Problems, Vol. 7, No. 1, 1959, pp. 40-47.

_____. "Sociology and Sociological Jurisprudence: Admixture of Lore and Law." Kentucky Law Journal, Vol. 52, Winter, 1964, pp. 267-293.

Gibbs, Jack P. "Crime and the Sociology of Law. Sociology and Social Research, Vol. 51, No. 1, October 1966.

_____. "The Sociology of Law and Normative Phenomena." American Sociological Review, Vol. 31, June 1966, pp. 315-325.

Gideon v. Wainright 372 U.S. 335 (1963).

Goebel, Jr., Julius. Felony and Misdemeanor A Study in the History of English Criminal Procedure. New York: The Commonwealth Fund, 1937.

Goff, Donald H. "An Interview." June 15, 1970, at The Correctional Association of New York.

Goffman, Erving. Asylums: Essays on the Social Situation of Mental Patients and Other Inmates. Garden City: Anchor Books, 1963.

Goldberg v. Kelly 397 U.S. (1970).

Goldfarb, Ronald. Ransom: A Critique of the American Bail System. New York: Harper and Row, 1965.

Goldkamp, John S. "Philadelphia Revisited: An Examination of Bail and Detention Two Decades After Foote." Crime and Delinquency, Vol. 26 (April 1980), pp. 179-192.

Goodman, Emily. "An Interview." April 21, 1971, at The Women's Bail Fund Headquarters, New York City.

Grand Jury Association of New York County. Preliminary Outline Regarding Bail in Criminal Actions. Prison Committee, Association of Grand Juries of New York County, Robert Appleton, Chairman. New York, 1925.

_____. Report Regarding the Practice of Fixing Bail Bonds. Prison Committee, Association of Grand Juries of New York County, Robert Appleton, Chairman. New York, 1925.

Grand Jury, Kings County, New York. A Presentation on The Execution of Bail Bonds. New York: Hamilton Press, 1941.

Green, Thomas. "Societal Concepts of Criminal Liability for Homicide in Medieval England." Speculum, Vol. XLVII, No. 4, October 1972, pp 669-695.

Griffin v. California 380 U.S. 609 (1965)

Griffin v. Illinois 351 U.S. 12 76 Supreme Court (1956)

Hamilton, Richard F. "The Marginal Middle Class: A Reconsideration." _American Sociological Review_, Vol. 31, No. 2, April 1966.

Hamilton v. Love 328 Fed. Supp. 1182 Eastern District Arkansas (1971).

Hanawalt, Barbara A. _Crime and Conflict in English Communities 1300-1348._ Cambridge, Mass.: Harvard University Press, 1979.

Harrison, A.R.W. _The Law of Athens: Procedure._ Oxford: Clarendon Press, 1971.

Harrison v. Stone 113 Florida, So (1934)

Hatt, Paul K. and Reiss, Albert J. _Cities and Societies_. New York: Free Press, 1957.

Hess, Albert and Thomas. "Incompetency to Stand Trial: Procedures, Results and Problems." 119 _American Journal of Psychiatry_, 713 (1963).

Hobson v. Hansen 269 Fed. Supp. Dist. of Columbia Circuit (1967).

Hohfeld, Wesley Newcomb. _Fundamental Legal Conceptions_. New Haven: Yale University Press, 1919.

"How the Church's Bail Fund Works." _Central Journal_, Fall 1972. New York: Central Presbyterian Church, N.P.

Hurnard, Naomi. _The King's Pardon for Homicide Before A.D. 1307_. New York: Oxford University Press, 1969.

Huttner, Richard D. "Bail Dilemma in Family Court." _New York Law Journal_, Vol. 184 (August 14, 1980), p. 2.

Ihering, Rudolf Ivan. _The Struggle for Law._ Trans. J.J. Lalor. Chicago: Callahan, 1897.

Insurance Vol. 27, Section 331 in _McKinney's Consolidated Laws of New York_, Brooklyn, N.Y.: Edward Thompson, 1963.

225

"Jail Census Finds 52% Not Convicted." The New York
    Times, January 7, 1971.

Jenks, Edward. Law and Politics in the Middle Ages.
    New York: Henry Holt, 1898.

Jennings, John. The Flow of Arrested Defendants
    Through New York City Criminal Court in 1968.
    New York: The Rand Institute, 1970.

_____. "An Interview." June 18, 1971, at the
    New York City Rand Corporation.

The Judiciary Act of 1789. 1 Stat. 91. Section 33.

"Judiciary and Jails Blamed by Panel for Tombs
    Suicide." The New York Times, November 18, 1970.

"Report on the Investigation of the Practices and
    Procedures in the Criminal Court of the City
    of New York." Judiciary Commission /Committee7
    of the New York Assembly, 1963.

"Judge Supported on Prostitution." The New York
    Times, August 1, 1971.

"Justice is Slow and Unsure in Nation's Busy Courts."
    The New York Times, Monday, March 8, 1971.

Kalven, Harry and Zeisel, Hans. The American Jury.
    Boston: Little Brown and Co., 1966.

Kantorowicz, Ernst H. "Savigny and the Historical
    School of Law." Law Quarterly Review, Vol. 53,
    pp. 326-343.

Kennedy, E.M. "New Approach to Bail Release: The
    Proposed Federal Criminal Code and Bail Reform."
    Fordham Law Review, Vol. 48, No. 4 (March 1980),
    pp. 423-436.

Kittrie, Nicholas. The Right to be Different.
    Baltimore: Johns Hopkins Press, 1971.

Kuh, Richard H. "Reflections on New York's Stop-and-
    Frisk Law and Its Claimed Unconstitutionality."
    Journal of Criminal Law, Criminology and Police
    Science, 56 (1965), p. 32f.

Langsdorff. "Is Bail a Rich Man's Privilege?"
Quotation 7, <u>Federal Rules and Decisions</u>,
pp. 309-310.

Lasswell, Harold D. and Arens, Richard. "The Role
of Sanction in Conflict Resolution." <u>Journal
of Conflict Resolution</u>, Vol. 11, No. 1, March
1967.

Lazar, Joseph. "Juridical Perspectives on National
Character." <u>Annals</u>, Vol. 370, March 1967.

Lenihan. <u>Measuring the Effect of a Bail Reform:
Manhattan Bail Reevaluation Project</u>. New York:
Vera Institute of Justice, N.D.

Littlefield, Neil O. "Eugen Ehrlich's Fundamental
Principles of the Sociology of Law." <u>Maine Law
Review</u>, Vol. 19, No. 1, 1967, p. 23.

Lockhart, Kamisar and Choper. <u>Cases and Materials on
Constitutional Acts and Liberties</u>. 3rd Edition.
St. Paul: West Publishing Co., 1970.

Maine, Sir Henry. <u>Ancient Law</u>. London: J. Murray,
1863.

"The Massachusetts Body of Liberties of 1641." In
<u>Annals of America</u>, Vol. 1, pp. 163-167. New York:
Encyclopedia Britannica, 1968.

Mattick, Hans W. "Foreword to 'The Future of
Imprisonment in a Free Society.'" <u>Key Issues</u>,
2:4-10, 1965.

McQuillan, Judge Peter. "An Interview." September 18,
1971 at New York City Criminal Court.

Mead, George H. "The Psychology of Primitive Justice."
<u>American Journal of Sociology</u>, Vol. 23, 1918,
pp. 577-602.

Menninger, Karl. <u>The Crime of Punishment</u>. New York:
Viking Press, Inc., 1968.

Merton, Robert K. <u>Social Theory and Social Structure</u>.
Rev. Ed. New York: Harcourt Brace and World,
1968.

Michael, Jerome and Adler, N.J. Crime, Law and Social Science. London: Kegan, Paul, Trench, Trubner and Cole, Ltd., 1933.

Millard v. Cameron 373 F 2nd Dist. of Columbia Circuit (1966).

Miller, Frank W. Prosecution: The Decision to Charge a Suspect With a Crime. Boston: Little Brown and Co., 1969.

Mills, C.W. "Structure of Power in American Society." British Journal of Sociology, Vol. 9, 1958, pp. 29-41.

Montesquieu, C.L. Baron De Secondat. The Spirit of the Laws. New York: Hafner Publishing Co., 1949.

Morris, Norval. Habitual Criminal. London: Longmans Green and Co., 1951.

_____ and Hawkins, G. Honest Politician's Guide to Crime Control. Chicago: University of Chicago Press, 1970.

Morris, Robert O. Decision-Making on Probation: A Study of Pre-Sentence Recommendations. University of California, Berkeley, Unpublished Doctoral Dissertation, 1969.

National Center for State Courts. An Evaluation of Policy Related Research on the Effectiveness of Pretrial Release Programs. Denver, Colorado: National Center for State Courts, 1975.

National Conference on Bail and Criminal Justice. Proceedings and Interim Report. New York: Institute on the Operation of Pretrial Release Projects, 1966.

Nelson, Benjamin. "Actors, Directors, Roles, Cues, Meanings, Identities: Further Thoughts on 'Anomie.'" The Psychoanalytic Review, Vol. 51, No. 1, Spring 1964, pp. 135-160.

_____. "Communities, Societies, Civilizations. Postmillenial Views on Masks and Faces of Change." Social Development, ed. by Manfred Stanley. New York: Basic Books, 1971.

_____. "Conscience and the Making of Early Modern Culture: The Protestant Ethic Beyond Max Weber." Social Research, Vol. 36, No. 1, Spring 1969, pp. 5-22.

_____. The Idea of Usury: From Tribal Brotherhood to Universal Otherhood. 2nd Edition Enlarged. Chicago: University of Chicago Press, 1969 (original 1949).

_____. "The Omnipresence of the Grotesque," Cultural Revolutions in the Generational Conflicts. Ed. Benjamin Nelson. Special issue of The Psychoanalytic Review, Vol. 57, No. 3, pp. 506-518.

Newman, Donald J. Conviction: The Determination of Guilt or Innocence Without Trial. Boston: Little Brown and Co., 1966.

_____. "Pleading Guilty for Considerations. The Study of Bargain Justice." Journal of Criminal Law, Criminology and Police Science, 46, March-April 1956, pp. 780-790.

Nimmes, Raymond T. The Nature of System Change. Chicago: American Bar Foundation, 1978.

The Nineteen Seventy-Two Criminal Justice Plan. New York: The Executive Committee of the Criminal Justice Coordinating Council, 1972.

Northrop, F.S.C. The Complexity of Legal and Ethical Experience. Boston: Little Brown and Co., 1959.

Oaks, Dallin H. and Lehman, Warren. Our Criminal Justice System and the Indigent. A Study of Chicago and Cook County. Chicago: The University of Chicago Press, 1968.

O'Meara, Charles. "An Interview." June 20, 1971, New York City Criminal Court.

Ombnibus Crime Control and Safe Streets Act of 1968. 18th United States Congress, No. 3501.

Ozanne, Marq R., Wilson, Robert A., Gedney, Dewaine L. "Toward a Theory of Bail Risk." Criminology, Vol. 18 (August 1980), pp. 147-161.

Parsons, Talcott. "The Law and Social Control."
In William N. Evan, ed., Law and Sociology:
Exploratory Essays. New York: Free Press, 1962.

_____, et al. Theories of Society. Vol. 1.
New York: Free Press, 1961.

Pearl, Michael. "Hard Times on Bail Bond Row."
New York, September 29, 1969, pp. 40-44.

Penal Law Vol. 39, Sections 100-219; 220-287 in
McKinney's Consolidated Laws of New York,
Brooklyn, N.Y.: Edward Thompson, 1968, ed.

People ex rel Lubell v. McDonnell 296 New York (1947).

People v. Calozzo 54 Misc. 2nd New York State 2nd
Supreme Court Kings County (1967).

Pistula, Kathy M. "Forcible Rape and the Right to
Bail." San Diego Law Review, Vol. 17 (August
1980), pp. 1061-1091.

"Police Drive Set on Bail Jumpers." New York Times,
January 6, 1971.

"The Politics of Jail Riots." The New York Post,
Wednesday, November 11, 1970.

Pollock, F. and Maitland, F.W. A History of English
Law Before the Time of Edward I. 2 volumes,
2nd edition with new introduction by S.F.C.
Milson. Cambridge: Cambridge University Press,
1968 (original 1895).

Pound, Roscoe. Criminal Justice in America. New York:
Henry Holt and Co., 1930.

_____. An Introduction to the Philosophy of Law.
New Haven: Yale University Press, 1922.

_____. The Scope and Subject Matter of the Law.
III in Jurisprudence, 5 volumes. St. Paul,
Minn.: West Publishing Co., 1959.

_____. Outline of Lectures on Jurisprudence.
Cambridge: Harvard University Press, 1928.

_____. Social Control Through Law. New Haven:
Yale University Press, 1942.

_____. A Theory of Social Interests. 15th
Proceedings of the American Sociological Society,
Vol. 16, 1921, pp. 29-30.

_____. In Criminal Justice, edited Sheldon Glueck.
Dobbs Ferry, N.Y.: Published for the National
Council on Crime and Delinquency by Oceana Press,
1965.

"Prisons Criticized by Vanden Heuvel." New York Times,
February 4, 1971.

Quinney, Richard, ed. Crime and Justice in Society.
Boston: Little Brown and Co., 1969.

Rankin, Anne. "The Effect of Pretrial Detention."
New York University Law Review, June 1964, No. 4,
pp. 641ff.

Reich, Charles. "The Law and the Corporate State."
In Sociological Readings and the Conflict
Perspective. Ed. W. Chambliss. Mass.: Addison-
Wesley Publishing Co., 1972, pp. 445-454.

Renner, Carl. The Institutions of Private Law and
Their Social Functions. O. Kahn Frund, ed.
Trans. A. Schwarzchild. London: Rutledge and
Kegan Paul, 1949.

Rheinstein, Max. Max Weber on Law and Economy in
Society. Trans. Shils and Rheinstein.
Cambridge: Harvard University Press, 1954.

Rose, Arnold M., ed. The Institutions of Advanced
Societies. Minneapolis, 1958.

Rose, A. "Some Suggestions for Research in the
Sociology of Law." Social Problems, Vol. 9,
No. 3, 1962, pp. 281-283.

Ross, David M. Administrative Judge of the Criminal
Court. "An Interview." January 21, 1971.

Ross, Edward A. Social Control. New York: Macmillan
Co., 1922.

F.S. Royster Guano Co. v. <u>Virginia</u> 253 U.S. (1920).

Rumble, Wilfred E. "Legal Realism, Sociological
    Jurisprodence and Mr. Justice Holmes." <u>Journal
    of History Ideas</u>, Vol. XXVI, October-December
    1965, pp. 547-66.

_____. "Rule, Skepticism and the Role of the Judge:
    A Study of American Legal Realism." <u>Journal of
    Public Law</u>, Vol. 15, No. 2, 1967.

Rusche, George and Kirchheimer, O. <u>Punishment and the
    Social Structure</u>. New York: Columbia University
    Press, 1939.

Savigny, Friedrich von. "Of the Vocation of Our Age
    for Legislation and Jurisprudence." In Cohen
    and Cohen, eds., <u>Readings in Jurisprudence and
    Legal Philosophy</u>. Englewood Cliffs, N.J.:
    Prentice Hall, 1951, pp. 388ff.

Sawyer, Geoffrey. <u>Law in Society</u>. London: Oxford
    University Press, 1965.

Schaffer, A. <u>Bail and Parole Jumping in Manhattan in
    1967</u>. New York: The Vera Institute of Justice,
    August 1970.

_____. "The Problem of Overcrowding in the
    Detention Institutions of New York City: An
    Analysis of Causes and Recommendations for
    Alleviation." Mimeograph. <u>A Report to the
    Mayor's Criminal Justice Coordinating Council</u>.
    New York: The Vera Institute of Justice, January
    1969, pp. 30-34.

Schur, Edwin M. <u>Law and Society. A Sociological View</u>.
    New York: Random House, 1968.

Selznick, Philip. "Legal Institutions and Social
    Controls." <u>Vanderbilt Law Review</u>, Vol. 17, 1963.

"Senate Approves 'Preventive Detention' Bill." <u>The
    New York Times</u>, Wednesday, December 9, 1981, A25.

<u>Shelton</u> v. <u>Tucker</u> 364 U.S. (1960).

Silverstein. "Bail and the State Courts - A Field
    Study and Report." 50 <u>Minnesota Law Review</u>,
    1966, pp. 621-631.

Sinclair, Kent. "Handling a Bail Application Under The Reform Act of 1966." National Law Journal, Vol. 2, June 2, 1980, p. 2.

Skolnick, Jerome H. Justice Without Trial. New York: John Wiley & Sons, Inc., 1966.

_____. "Sociology of Law in America: Overview and Trends." Social Problems, Vol. 13, Summer 1965, p. 4ff.

Small, Albion W. General Sociology. New York: Appleton & Co., 1905.

Smith, T.B. "Bail Before Trial. Reflections of a Scottish Lawyer." 108 University of Pennsylvania Law Review, 1960.

"Speed Crime Trials or Quash Charges." New York Times, January 6, 1971.

"State Senate Committee Charges City Lags on Proposals for Reforms at Tombs." New York Times, Thursday, February 4, 1971.

Stenton, D.N., ed. Rolls of the Justices in Eyre, Being Rolls of Pleas and Assizes for Lincolnshire 1218-19 and Worcestershire, 1221. London: 1934.

Stone, Julius. The Province and Function of Law. Cambridge: Harvard University Press, 1961.

Subin, Harry, Professor of Law, New York University. "An Interview." August 1971.

Sudnow, David. "Normal Crimes: Sociological Features of the Penal Code and the Public Defender Office." Social Problems, 12 Winter 1965, pp. 255-276.

Suffet, Frederic. "Bail Setting: A Study of Court-room Interaction." New York: The Vera Institute of Justice (reprint) 1965.

_____. "Patterns of Failure to Raise Bail." Unpublished manuscript of the Vera Foundation, 1965.

"Supreme Court, 5-4, Bars Death Penalty As It Is Imposed Under Present Statutes." New York Times, June 30, 1972, p. 1.

Tate v. Short 401 U.S. (1971).

Thomas, Arthur E. "Community Power and Student Rights." Harvard Educational Review, Vol. 42, No. 2, May 1972, pp. 173-216.

Timasheff, N.S. An Introduction to the Sociology of Law. Cambridge: Harvard University Press, 1939.

Tocqueville, Alexis de. Democracy in America. Ed. by J.P. Mayer, Trans. George Lawrence. Garden City: Doubleday Anchor Books, 1969.

"Tombs Prisoners Seize Five Hostages in Eight-Hour Protest." New York Times, August 10, 1970.

Tompkins, Dorothy C. Bail in the United States: A Bibliography. Berkeley Calif.: Institute for Governmental Studies, 1966.

_____. The Confession Issue - From McNabb to Miranda: A Bibliography. Berkeley Calif.: Institute for Governmental Studies. 1966.

_____. The Offender - A Bibliography. Berkeley, Calif.: Institute for Governmental Studies, 1963.

Troia, Virginia K. "Voluntary Detention vs. Seizure of a Person." Creighton Law Review, Vol. 14, (Summer 1981), pp. 1138-1144.

Turk, Austin T. "Conflict and Criminality." American Sociological Review, Vol. 31, No. 3, June 1966.

"Two Held Without Bail in Prostitution Case By An Angry Judge." New York Times, Wednesday, July 7, 1971.

Uniform Crime Reports - 1969. Washington, D.C.: United States Department of Justice, 1970-1971.

United States v. Alston 420 F 2nd Dist. of Columbia Circuit (1969).

United States v. Bandy 81 Supreme Court (1970).

234

United States v. Brawner 7 Fed Western District,
    Tennessee (1851).

United States Congress Federal Bail Reform Act. 18th
    Congress, No. ﾠ146.

United States v. Forrest 418 F 2nd Dist. of Columbia
    Circuit (1969).

United States v. Lawrence 26 Federal Case No. 15577
    Circuit Court Dist. of Columbia (1835).

United States v. Rumrich 180 Fed 2nd Second Circuit
    (1950).

"United States To Seek Changes In Criminal Sentencing."
    New York Times, Tuesday, November 10, 1970.

'United States v. Dohm and the Compelled Election
    Between the Right to Remain Silent and the Right
    to Reasonable Bail." Harvard Law Review, Case
    Note. Vol. 94 (December 1980), pp. 426-438.

U.S. Task Force Assessment of Crime. Task Force
    Report: Crime and Its Impact. An Assessment.
    President's Commission on Law Enforcement and
    the Administration of Justice, U.S. Government
    Printing Office, 1967.

Vanden Heuvel, William, Commissioner of the Board of
    Correction. "An Interview." October 1971 at
    the Offices of Struuk, Struuk and Lavan.

Viorst, M., ed. Great Documents of Western
    Civilization. New York: Chilton Books, 1965.

Wainwright, Cynthia, ed. Department of Correction
    Bail Re-evaluation Project. Final Report. New
    York: Fund for the City of New York, August 1972.

"Waiting for Their Day in Court - Can - and Does -
    Take Many Months in Jail." The New York Times,
    Sunday, December 6, 1970.

Wald, Patricia. "Pretrial Detention and Ultimate
    Freedom." New York University Law Review, Vol.
    39, June 1964, No. 4.

Ward, Lester F. Applied Sociology. Boston: Ginn,
    1906.

_____. Dynamic Sociology. New York: D. Appleton and Co., 1883.

Weber, Max. "Formal and Substantive Rationalization of the Law," in S.N. Eisenstadt, ed., Max Weber on Charisma and Institution Building. Chicago: University of Chicago Press, 1968.

_____. The Protestant Ethic and the Spirit of Capitalism. New York: Free Press, 1963.

_____. The Theory of Social and Economic Organization. Parsons, ed. New York: Oxford University Press, 1947.

Weintraub, Judith, Assistant General Secretary of The Correctional Association of New York. "An Interview." June 15, 1970. At The Correctional Association of New York.

Wilkins, L.T. Social Deviants. New Jersey: Prentice Hall, 1964.

_____. "Values versus Variables - An Essay on the Relevance of Measurement to Morals and Value Judgements." Crime and Culture, ed. Wolfgang, p. 146.

Williams v. Illinois 399 U.S. (1970).

"Wisconsin Bail Reform." Wisconsin Law Review, No. 2, 1971, pp. 594-604.

Wolfgang, Marvin. Patterns in Criminal Homicide. Philadelphia: University of Pennsylvania Press, 1958.

Wood, A.L. "Professional Ethics Among Criminal Lawyers." Social Problems, Vol. 7, No. 1, 1959, p. 70f.

Zeisel, Hans. "Methodological Problems and Techniques in Sociological Research." Law and Society Review, Vol. 2, No. 3, May 1968.

_____. Bail Revisited. Chicago: American Bar Foundation, 1979.

INDEX

BAIL IN CRIMINAL COURT: NEW YORK

237

238

240

Drug Enforcement Administration, 206-207

District of Columbia *Criminal Code*, 205

due process, 18, 189

Durkheim, Emile, 3, 65

Edward I, 3

employment:
  bail, pretrial release and, 161-164
  post-arrest outcome and, 164-165

equal protection, 18-19, 31

Escobedo v. *Illinois*, 189

excessive bail, 55-56, 66

Federal Rules of Criminal Procedure, 17, 56, 77-78, 186, 205

Feliciano, Jose, 51

Foote, Caleb, 13, 26, 57, 58, 63, 65, 179, 186

Frankfurter, Felix, 16

frankpledge, 4-5

Freund, Paul A., 78-79

Furman v. *Georgia*, 190

Gamelyn Romance, 10

Geis, G., 20

Georgia; Furman v., 190

Gideon v. *Wainwright*, 189

Gierke, Otton Von, 4

Goffman, Erving, 52, 63, 179

Goldberg, Justice Arthur, 189

CRIMINAL JUSTICE BUDGET 1970-1971

			%
1.	Police Patrol	$421,746,297	(51.2)
2.	Crime Investigation	103,333,643	(12.3)
3.	Traffic Law Enforcement	55,947,413	(6.6)
4.	Confinement	55,733,246	(6.6)
5.	Support	34,467,123	(4.1)
6.	Drug Addiction Treatment	30,779,752	(3.7)
7.	Debt Service	30,360,197	(3.6)
8.	Adjudication	28,382,768	(3.4)
9.	Administration	20,357,556	(2.4)
10.	Probation Services (including ROR)	17,156,065	(2.0)
11.	Emergency Police Service	13,038,127	(1.5)
12.	Prosecution of Offenders	8,966,309	(1.1)
13.	Medical/Mental Health Services	7,077,798	(0.8)
14.	Defense of Offenders	4,000,000	(0.4)
15.	Rehabilitation Programs	2,518,018	(0.3)
	TOTAL	$843,208,910	

APPENDIX A

248